Food Culture in the Caribbean

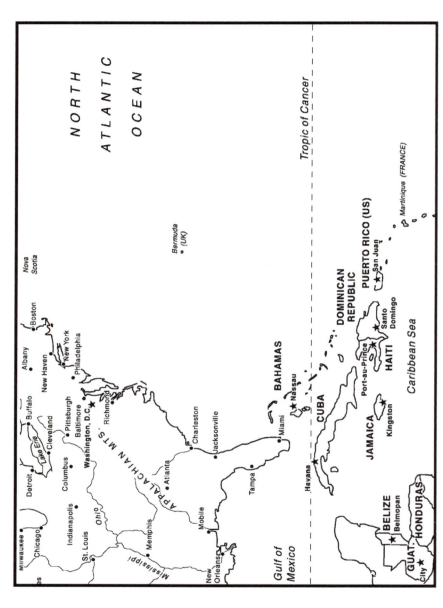

Caribbean. Cartography by Mapcraft.com.

Food Culture in the
Caribbean

LYNN MARIE HOUSTON

Food Culture around the World

Ken Albala, Series Editor

GREENWOOD PRESS

Westport, Connecticut   ·   London

Library of Congress Cataloging-in-Publication Data

Houston, Lynn Marie.
    Food culture in the Caribbean / Lynn Marie Houston.
        p. cm. — (Food culture around the world, ISSN 1545–2638)
    Includes bibliographical references and index.
    ISBN 0–313–32764–5 (alk. paper)
    1. Cookery, Caribbean. 2. Food habits—Caribbean Area. I. Title. II. Series.
TX716.A1H67   2005
394.1´2´09729—dc22   2005003393

British Library Cataloguing in Publication Data is available.

Library of Congress Catalog Card Number: 2005003393
ISBN: 0–313–32764–5
ISSN: 1545–2638

First published in 2005

Greenwood Press, 88 Post Road West, Westport, CT 06881
An imprint of Greenwood Publishing Group, Inc.
www.greenwood.com

Printed in the United States of America

The paper used in this book complies with the
Permanent Paper Standard issued by the National
Information Standards Organization (Z39.48–1984).

10 9 8 7 6 5 4 3 2 1

Illustrations by J. Susan Cole Stone.

The publisher has done its best to make sure the instructions and/or recipes in this book
are correct. However, users should apply judgment and experience when preparing recipes, especially parents and teachers working with young people. The publisher accepts no
responsibility for the outcome of any recipe included in this volume.

Contents

Series Foreword

The appearance of the Food Culture around the World series marks a definitive stage in the maturation of Food Studies as a discipline to reach a wider audience of students, general readers, and foodies alike. In comprehensive interdisciplinary reference volumes, each on the food culture of a country or region for which information is most in demand, a remarkable team of experts from around the world offers a deeper understanding and appreciation of the role of food in shaping human culture for a whole new generation. I am honored to have been associated with this project as series editor.

Each volume follows a series format, with a chronology of food-related dates and narrative chapters entitled Introduction, Historical Overview, Major Foods and Ingredients, Cooking, Typical Meals, Eating Out, Special Occasions, and Diet and Health. Each also includes a glossary, bibliography, resource guide, and illustrations.

Finding or growing food has of course been the major preoccupation of our species throughout history, but how various peoples around the world learn to exploit their natural resources, come to esteem or shun specific foods and develop unique cuisines reveals much more about what it is to be human. There is perhaps no better way to understand a culture, its values, preoccupations and fears, than by examining its attitudes toward food. Food provides the daily sustenance around which families and communities bond. It provides the material basis for rituals through which people celebrate the passage of life stages and their connection to divinity.

Food preferences also serve to separate individuals and groups from each other, and as one of the most powerful factors in the construction of identity, we physically, emotionally and spiritually become what we eat.

By studying the foodways of people different from ourselves we also grow to understand and tolerate the rich diversity of practices around the world. What seems strange or frightening among other people becomes perfectly rational when set in context. It is my hope that readers will gain from these volumes not only an aesthetic appreciation for the glories of the many culinary traditions described, but also ultimately a more profound respect for the peoples who devised them. Whether it is eating New Year's dumplings in China, folding tamales with friends in Mexico or going out to a famous Michelin-starred restaurant in France, understanding these food traditions helps us to understand the people themselves.

As globalization proceeds apace in the twenty-first century it is also more important than ever to preserve unique local and regional traditions. In many cases these books describe ways of eating that have already begun to disappear or have been seriously transformed by modernity. To know how and why these losses occur today also enables us to decide what traditions, whether from our own heritage or that of others, we wish to keep alive. These books are thus not only about the food and culture of peoples around the world, but also about ourselves and who we hope to be.

Ken Albala
University of the Pacific

Acknowledgments

Consuming authentic Caribbean food can be an emotionally moving experience, not only in terms of the euphoria caused by its fresh ingredients, intense flavors, and spicy seasonings, but also in the awareness that diverse groups of people have had to come together in various state of contentment and discontentment in order to produce even just a morsel of a Caribbean meal. It is with this modest, somewhat clichéd idea—of people getting together through good times and bad—that I began and wrote this book on Caribbean food. The historical content of this book, explaining what we know of the diet of indigenous peoples through the chronicles of European invaders, the descriptions of many fruits and vegetables that have found their way from all around the world to become essential ingredients in Caribbean cuisine, and the outlines of typical meals or meals for special occasions in the various islands and the corresponding recipes, all honor the diverse peoples who have left their mark on Caribbean food culture, which, in turn, has transformed the food culture of the entire world.

In the same vein, the writing and publication of this book honors the people who have had a hand in shaping my ideas on food, culture, and the Caribbean, as well as those who have provided support of other kinds. Acknowledgment for their assistance follows.

First and foremost, I am indebted to other scholars of food and culture, those whose work has preceded mine in the areas of women's food culture and foodways of, in, and around the Caribbean: Carole Counihan, Olive

Senior, Sidney Mintz, Jessica B. Harris, Cristine Mackie, John Demers, Rosamund Grant, Elisabeth Rozin, Doris Witt, Angela Shelf Medearis, Diane Spivey, and others too numerous to name. I am grateful as well to the exchanges with friends and colleagues involved with the Popular Culture and American Culture Association (PCA/ACA), especially the Southwest region of this organization. A big thank you goes to Marjorie Gardner of the School of Hospitality & Tourism at the University of Technology in Jamaica, whose research on Jamaican street foods, presented at the 2004 PCA/ACA national conference, was indispensable to Chapter 5 of this book. Thanks also to the Association of the Study of Food and Society (ASFS) for the enrichment their publications, conferences, and listserv have provided. A special thanks goes to members of the ASFS listserv who responded with information to questions I posted there about Caribbean food culture, particularly Pamela Lewy, Jeffrey Miller, Sarah Venable, Alison Ross, and Annie Hauck-Lawson.

I cannot praise highly enough Ken Albala, the series editor, and Wendi Schnaufer, the series contact at Greenwood Press. They deserve thanks not only for their assistance in the steps of researching, writing, and revising this book, but also for being gracious mentors from whom I have learned much. Wendi Schnaufer's editing of this manuscript was nothing short of genius. I would also like to thank Apex Publishing for guiding my book through the production process.

At Tulane University's Latin American library, I would like to thank the library's director, Hortensia Calvo, and reference librarian Paul Bary, for their assistance in my research, especially during their library's remodeling. At the Tulane University Medical Library, I would like to thank Cynthia Goldstein, Barbara Volo, and the rest of the staff for being so accommodating and helpful.

I want to acknowledge those friends, colleagues, and former professors who were involved with my early forays into Caribbean literature and food. Thanks to the host of people who befriended me during my time at the University of Geneva for educating me in various cultural traditions and sharing my love of food (especially Marie Fellay Guhirwa). Thanks also to those professors who were instrumental in the course my studies have taken into the field of Caribbean food culture: during my time at Hartwick College, David Jeffres, Margaret Schramm, and Ann Hibner Koblitz; while at the University of Geneva, Wlad Godzich, Paul Taylor, and Richard Waswo; and during my studies at Arizona State University, Myriam Chancy, Peter Goggin, Ellen Rees, Mark Lussier, Devoney Looser, and Arturo Aldama. Special thanks go to these latter three mentors for their hard work in seeing me through my doctoral studies and for believing wholeheartedly in my work. I have been blessed with similar support for my food studies scholarship from my new colleagues in the English department at California State University, Chico.

I could not have written this without the encouragement from friends who encouraged me: Ann Evans, Don Fette, Ayona Datta, Shawn and Donna Murray of Spicy Productions, and Jason and Michelle Harris. Thanks to those who taste-tested the recipes from this book when I made them and gave me constructive feedback. I would like to thank my co-workers at Golden and Fonte law firm for discussions about food and for some time off to write this book. I would especially like to thank John Kopfinger, who shared with me his vast knowledge of Caribbean cooking and even lent me cookbooks from his private collection.

Barclay, the best cat in the world, also warrants special mention for his unconditional love and affection. He was either at my side or on my lap from the beginning to the end of this project.

I dedicate this book to my family. A large part of Caribbean food culture is, after all, about celebrating ancestral and familial ties. For the values they instilled in me, for their continual support, and their extreme generosity, I dedicate these pages especially to my mother and father. I thank them and the rest of my family for their love and encouragement.

May God bless you all and grant us many more opportunities to place food and drink at the service of making the time we spend together all the more memorable.

Introduction

As European voyagers first encountered the islands of the Caribbean on the expeditions led by Spanish explorer Christopher Columbus, they were so awed by the lush, tropical vegetation that they thought they had found the Garden of Eden described in the Bible. The geography and climate of the Caribbean still evoke this comparison from many travelers. Like early European explorers, some tourists today come to the Caribbean with a lack of knowledge about its peoples, customs, and cultures, and instead perceive their experiences in Caribbean countries from within their own cultural attitudes and values. The development of a whitewashed tourist culture and resort system prompted by affordable and reliable air transportation since the 1950s has made it even harder for the traveler to learn about Caribbean culture by experiencing the everyday life of Caribbean people. This book hopes to serve as a reference source for those who want to go beyond the typical tourist's experience and learn about Caribbean history and culture through a thorough examination of Caribbean food culture and the issues affecting Caribbean food production.

This book also attempts to help situate the Caribbean within the context of the Americas by hinting at the connections that the Caribbean, South America, and North America share through foodways (through the ways in which the people of these regions come to select, prepare, and consume foods, as well as the social and cultural meanings behind their agricultural systems, food choices, preparation styles, and eating behaviors). The Caribbean, once an important center for European commerce, has more recently become a strategic location within the Americas due to similar trade issues. This role is complicated by the U.S. perspective, since the 1823 Monroe Doctrine, of the Caribbean as its backyard. In this respect, the territory of the Caribbean shares much with Latin America, but Spanish-speaking territories in the Caribbean often are excluded from studies on the Caribbean because they are considered part of Latin America, and, thus, not important to understanding the Caribbean. However, the movement of goods within the Americas demands more of an inclusive approach.

Caribbean culture has always been enmeshed with the stakes of trade and commerce through its territory. The name of the country Puerto Rico in Spanish literally means "rich port." Internet searches for information about Caribbean cultural traditions using the keywords "Caribbean customs" brings up sites for "customs and port authorities," and many other searches for information regarding the Caribbean bring up commercial sites for cruise ships disguised as informative sources about Caribbean culture. From the time of European exploration, the Caribbean's role in global trade and commerce has centered on consumable goods.

As a significant site in the trade and commerce of foods in the Americas, food culture of the Caribbean has greatly affected the rest of the world. Consider what other world cuisines would look like without the foods discovered by European explorers in the Americas and taken to other parts of the globe: think of Irish cooking without potatoes, Italian cuisine without tomatoes, Asian and African cooking without hot peppers, and no peanuts, corn, or chocolate anywhere. This exchange was not one-sided, however, as many cultures from around the world have also affected the Caribbean, bringing with them their own foods and cooking styles, as well as their religions, customs, and languages. In fact, one of the biggest challenges to eating in the Caribbean is a linguistic one: recognizing the various names of food items and dishes. One food or dish can be called a different name in English, Spanish, French, Dutch, Hindi, and Chinese, and have yet a different name in some of the Creole languages like English Creole (a blend of English and African languages spoken in Jamaica), French Creole (a blend of French and African languages spoken in Haiti), patois (a mixture of English, Spanish, and French), and Papiamento (a mixture of Dutch, Portuguese, Spanish, English, and African languages spoken in Aruba, Bonaire, and Curacao).

Because the Caribbean cultural identity has been formed from the diverse languages, customs, and traditions of immigrants from all over the world who have come to settle in the Caribbean, many writers find a metaphor for Caribbean culture in the widely popular Caribbean stew dish called Callaloo. Like other aspects of Caribbean culture, the history of food in the Caribbean and its relationship to the Caribbean identity is also similar to the nature of a pot of stew: different ethnic groups maintain their food customs and traditions (standing out like the visibly recognizable pieces of meat and vegetables in a stew), but at the same time these food customs and traditions have altered (and been altered by) the customs and traditions of other ethnic groups present in the Caribbean, so that like the ingredients in a stew, after sitting together in a pot for a few hours, the individual ingredients tend to lose their individual flavors and blend together to create a new, distinct flavor. Just like in many other multicultural areas of the world, individual ethnicities in the Caribbean blend together; however, while the contours of their customs may be blurred, they are not completely erased.

GEOGRAPHY AND CLIMATE

The Caribbean region is a chain of islands running from off the coast of Florida to Venezuela. It is also known as the West Indies because of the mistaken conception on the part of the first European explorers of this region that the islands were actually part of the Orient. The list of countries that belong to the region labeled the Caribbean is nebulous and inexact, because while some countries are not necessarily situated within the Caribbean Sea (for example, some countries border it), they are nonetheless culturally Caribbean. Usually, the territory is divided up into the Greater Antilles, the Lesser Antilles, and the Bahamas (which includes Turks and Caicos islands). The Greater Antilles includes Cuba, the Cayman Islands, Hispaniola (the island shared by Haiti and the Dominican Republic), Jamaica, and Puerto Rico. The Lesser Antilles comprise two groups of islands called the Windward Islands and the Leeward Islands (whose names are based on the prevailing direction of winds), plus the eastern Caribbean islands. Dominica, Martinique, St. Lucia, Barbados, St. Vincent, and the Grenadines make up the Windward Islands. The U.S. and British Virgin Islands, Anguilla, St. Maarten/St. Martin, St. Barthelemy, Saba, St. Eustatius, St. Kitts, Nevis, Antigua, Barbuda, Montserrat, and Guadeloupe make up the Leeward Islands. Remaining islands in the southeastern and southwestern Caribbean Sea are Grenada, Trinidad and Tobago, other small islands off the coast of Venezuela, and the Netherlands Antilles group: Aruba, Bonaire, and Curacao. In 2003, the population of these combined territories was approximately 37 million.

The Caribbean has a great diversity of landscapes housing its very diverse populations. From mountainous regions, volcanoes, and rainforests to deserts and beaches, islands in the Caribbean have very distinct natural environments. Even the use of individual parcels of land within Caribbean countries, sometimes even neighboring plots, exhibit great diversity: for example, the large, mechanized sugar plantation bordered by small land holdings of nonmechanized subsistence farmers. All of the Caribbean islands, however, are united by the tropical climate that they share in common. Temperatures are warm year-round, varying only by about ten degrees between the average mean temperatures for summer and winter, which means that tropical crops like beans, peas, cucumber, tomato, cabbage, cauliflower, carrot, peppers, yams, cassava, breadfruit, spinach, passion fruit, and limes are grown throughout the Caribbean. Hurricane season for the entire Caribbean is from June through October. The dry season is from November to February.

The tourist industry has now also become a unifying factor among the diverse lands of the Caribbean, and the building of hotels and resorts has affected the geography of the region. During mid-December to mid-April, the heaviest tourist season in the Caribbean, North Americans seek refuge on Caribbean beaches from wintertime temperatures at home. During the off-season, however, many Caribbean peoples themselves explore their neighboring regions, and Europeans vacation there as well. Some tourist facilities close during August and September and possibly even October.

RELIGION

Like the different languages spoken throughout the Caribbean, religion is predominantly determined by ethnic, racial, and cultural heritage. In the Dutch Caribbean, for instance, Caribbean people are mainly Catholic, although there is a small percentage of Caribbeans who have emigrated from the Eastern Caribbean who are Protestant. Anglo people, or those of European descent, are likely to be Protestant or Jewish. In the Eastern Caribbean, as in Trinidad, local whites are known as French Creoles and are predominantly Catholic. Other whites of British descent are more likely to be Protestant. Trinidad has a large population of immigrants from India who mainly practice Hinduism, with a smaller Islamic population. Presbyterian missionaries in the early twentieth century worked among the Indian population, so it is not uncommon to find a small portion of Trinidadians practicing Presbyterianism. Most Caribbean people recognize Christian religious celebrations, although they may never attend a Christian religious service. The African influence in the Caribbean has also contributed significantly to religious practices such as Orisha, practiced today mainly in Trinidad and also in Grenada, and Obeah. Blends of African religions with Christianity have produced a number of religions in the Caribbean as well: Vodun, or Vodou (which comes from Benin on the west coast of Africa) in Haiti and Santeria (which comes from the Yoruban peoples of West Africa) in Cuba, the Dominican Republic, and Puerto Rico. These religions are known as syncretistic because they show examples of a blend of religions, specifically a blend of indigenous African spiritual practices with Christian influences from colonial powers. The Rastafarian movement, championed popularly by the late reggae master Bob Marley, is a spiritual and political movement indigenous to Jamaica but founded on many principles of African religious beliefs and Hinduism. In general, scholars summarize Christian religions in the Caribbean by characterizing the Spanish and French Caribbean islands as Catholic, and the British and Dutch Caribbean islands as Protestant; however, they note that in addition to these official religions, for many people, religious practices that blend influences of multiple religions and that draw from folk traditions are the norm.

THE CARIBBEAN BY REGIONS

In this book, discussions of the Caribbean are broken up into regions of colonial influence: British, French, Spanish, and Dutch. This is not to suggest that in any way these Caribbean territories should continue to be defined by the colonial powers that once controlled them (or the ones that still do), but that the food culture of these regions has been distinctively marked by European settlement and colonial influences and reflects the blending of European food cultures with immigrant and indigenous food cultures. Often, too, official articulations of culture are still linked to the European colonial past. In the following section, distinctions between European colonial powers are not always clear, as Britain, Spain, France, and the Netherlands fought over control of islands in the Caribbean and many islands changed hands over the course of history.

Interisland connections have been forged along the lines of European colonial influences and along linguistic lines, which often go hand in hand. The shared Caribbean historical heritage—in general, moving from European settlement and decimation of indigenous population, importation of African slaves, emancipation of slaves and importation of indentured servants from Asia, independence from colonial forces and emigration, and increasing reliance on tourism—is discussed in relevance to issues impacting food culture, in Chapter 1.

The next introductory section gives background on the history of the political situations and populations in Caribbean territories. The section is broken down by major regions because many islands in these regions share very similar historical, political, and economic characteristics. While not every island in the Caribbean is covered, the major islands and countries defining the regions are addressed.

The British Caribbean

The British-influenced Caribbean extends to the islands of Anguilla, Antigua and Barbuda, the Bahamas, Barbados, Bermuda, the Cayman Islands, Dominica, Grenada, Montserrat, St. Kitts and Nevis, St. Lucia, St. Vincent, Trinidad and Tobago, Turks and Caicos, and the Virgin Islands. When referred to as the Commonwealth Caribbean, this region also includes the mainland countries of Belize and Guyana. These territories are managed by such organizations as the Caribbean Community and Common Market (Caricom) (at which Haiti and the Dominican Republic are included as observers but not active participants), and the Organization of Eastern Caribbean States (OECS).

Anguilla

Anguilla is a dependent territory under British rule. Its people are mainly of African descent. The official language is English and the main religions are Anglican and Methodist. Anguilla used to be considered a single colony with St. Kitts (otherwise known as St. Christopher) and Nevis, but when it tried to declare its independence from these other islands it went back to British control.

Antigua and Barbuda

The people of Antigua and Barbuda are mainly of African descent. Most of the population lives in the city of St. John's. Barbuda is a coral island off the coast of Antigua. The official language of both territories is English. Barbuda presents a rare example of national development for the Caribbean, as its lands were never used to cultivate sugarcane; its people have always, instead, gained their living by fishing and subsistence farming. Antigua was colonized by the British in 1632, while Barbuda was not colonized until 1678. In 1834, Britain emancipated the slaves in these two territories. Antigua became fully independent in 1981.

Bahamas

The name of the Bahamas comes from the Spanish word *bajamar* meaning shallow seas. Its population is made up of people of African descent, but there are also some British, Greek, and Syrian descendants, as well as Haitians and other West Indians. English is the native language in the Bahamas, but with an influx of Haitian immigrants one can hear French and French Creole being spoken. The Bahamas achieved independence from Britain in 1973.

Barbados

About 90 percent of the population of Barbados is of African descent. The rest of the population is made up of those with European descent and mixed European and African heritage, as well as East Indians. English is the official language, but a Creole English called Bajan is spoken by many. Barbados achieved independence from Britain in 1966 and has one of the most stable political systems in the English Caribbean. Much of its farmland is held by large estates on which peasants work in a system of tenant farming.

Dominica

Dominica was named by Columbus; he saw the island on a Sunday and named it after the Latin *dies dominica*, or the Lord's day. Dominica went back and forth between French and British colonial control for many decades, but it became independent in 1978. Its population is mainly of African descent, but Dominica also has one of the largest population of Carib descendants in the area. While English is the official language, French patois is spoken, and many place names are derived from Carib words. Dominica is a rather poor country and lacks the tourist facilities of most of the other Caribbean islands. It has had a recent history of extremely devastating hurricanes. In 1979, Hurricane David almost destroyed the entire agricultural system of the island, washing away most of its topsoil.

Jamaica

Columbus named this island Santiago, but it has since reclaimed a derivation of its indigenous name *Xaymaca* (meaning land of wood and water). The British seized Jamaica from Spain in 1655 and, in the process, the existent slaves fled into the mountains. There they formed communities, living in the fierce wilderness, and became known as the Maroons (derived from the Spanish word *cimarrón*, meaning wild or untamed. During British occupation, other slaves joined these communities until they were emancipated in 1833. In 1930, Marcus Garvey became an outspoken labor leader and led a revolt to change conditions for the working class. Jamaica achieved independence in 1962 and has become a commonwealth. Jamaica's population is predominately Afro-Caribbean and mulatto descendants of slaves, with small communities of British, Indians, Chinese, Syrians, Portuguese, and Germans. English is the official language, but English Creole (a mix of English, African languages, Spanish, and even French) is widely spoken. Fishing is a major way of life, supporting some 150,000 people.

St. Kitts and Nevis

Although Columbus named one of these islands St. Christopher after his patron saint, the name was shortened later by British colonists to St. Kitts. The name Nevis comes from Columbus's description of the clouds on the island's mountains as *las nieves* or snowy. St. Kitts and Nevis are two islands that have been considered, together, as a sovereign state since achieving independence in 1983. Their population is mainly of African descent with a small percentage of mulattos, east Indians, and white Europeans.

St. Lucia

Both the French and the British vied for control of this island during the seventeenth and eighteenth centuries, and it exchanged hands many times. Although it is considered part of the English-influenced Caribbean, achieving independence from Britain in 1979, the French influence can be seen in the popularly spoken French patois (despite the official language being English) and the high percentage of Roman Catholics. Its population consists of a majority of Afro-Caribbeans, with a small mulatto, white European, and east Indian population.

Virgin Islands

The Virgin Islands are broken up into the U.S. islands, which are a territory of the United States, and the British islands, which were a former British colony. The U.S. group is made up of St. Croix, St. Thomas, and St. John, while the British group is made up of, most notably, Tortola, Virgin Gorda, and Anegada. The population of the Virgin Islands is mainly descendants of African slaves, but immigration from Puerto Rico and from the mainland United States has increased the population in recent years. Descendants of French Huguenots make up a distinct ethnic group and are called the Chachas. The official language is English, but a dialect termed Calypso is spoken. Also, French is spoken on St. Thomas and some Spanish is spoken on St. Croix, which has a large Puerto Rican immigrant population.

Trinidad and Tobago

The islands of Trinidad and Tobago together constitute an independent republic since winning independence from Britain in 1962. The set of islands are linguistically diverse. While English is the official language, some east Indian languages are spoken and there are also four different Creole languages spoken popularly: Trinidad English, French Creole, Spanish Creole, and Manzanillan, a mix of English, Spanish, and several different African languages.

The French Caribbean

The French Caribbean includes Haiti and the islands of Guadeloupe, Martinique, St. Barth, and St. Martin (the French side) in the Eastern Caribbean. Sometims the South American island of French Guyana is even considered part of the French Caribbean.

Haiti

Haiti occupies the western third of the island of Hispaniola, shared with the Dominican Republic. The Treaty of Rijswijk gave the land to France from Spain, and the French named it Saint-Domingue. A slave rebellion started in the 1790s gave Haiti its independence in 1804, making it the first black republic in the Americas, and the second country in the Americas, after the United States, to gain freedom from colonial rule. Haiti's independence was achieved partly due to progress made by Toussaint-Louverture, a former slave, who had become governor in 1801, but a black army formed by Jean-Jacques Dessalines and Henri Christophe achieved the final victory over the French. After independence, the Taino name Haiti, meaning mountainous land, was reclaimed. In 1822, Santo Domingo (the Dominican Republic) was invaded by Haiti, but by 1844 they had been expelled; Haiti and neighboring Dominican Republic have had a rather violent history of cohabitation. The Haitian government it-self is characterized by a history of popular uprisings and assassinations of political leaders. In 1957, François Duvalier (known as Papa Doc) became president and enacted a police state, declaring himself president for life. Toward the end of his life, he designated his son, Jean-Claude, known as Baby Doc, as the next president. His time in office was ended by a popular uprising in 1986. In 1990, Jean-Bertrand Aristide was elected in the first free elections in Haiti but was ousted the next year by the military. After the United States imposed a trade embargo, tens of thousands of Haitians attempted to flee the country to the United States by boat. Aristide returned in 1994, served his term until 1996, and was reelected in 2000. In the beginning of 2004, popular uprisings again forced Aristide to give up his office and flee the country.

Most Haitians are of African descent. Like the majority of areas in the Caribbean, most of Haiti's natural landscape has been lost due to practices of agriculture, grazing, and timber production. Haiti's culture is what is known as Creole, a mixture of Western and African influences; it shares this distinct culture with other islands like Guadeloupe, Dominica, Martinique, and St. Lucia. Its official languages are Haitian Creole and French. Unlike many other Caribbean countries, malaria is still a major health problem for Haitians. Many lack proper medical treatment as Haiti is one of the economically poorest countries in the Western Hemisphere. Its material culture, however, is rich.

Guadeloupe

Guadeloupe is an overseas department of France. The Carib name for the land was *karukera*, meaning island of beautiful waters. Colonial control of the island went back and forth between the French and the British. In 1703, Jean-Baptiste Labat led slaves in armed revolt against British occupation and helped bring the island to prosperity by founding sugar refineries there. Emancipation for slaves was achieved in 1848. The population of Guadeloupe is mainly Creole of mixed European and African descent. St. Barth and St. Martin are dependencies of Guadeloupe and have a larger white European population. French is the official language, but Creole is also spoken.

Martinique

Martinique is also an overseas department of France. Its name comes from the Carib words *madiana* or *madinina*: meaning, respectively, island of flowers or fertile island with luxuriant vegetation. The Dutch and the English both fought the French over possession of Martinique, and the island went back and forth between French and British control during colonial times. Slaves in Martinique were emancipated in 1848. In 1902, an active volcano, Mount Pelée, erupted and killed 30,000 people. Most of the population of Martinique is mulatto, but white Creoles hold the economic power. The official language is French, but a Creole dialect similar to that of Haiti is spoken.

The Spanish Caribbean

Countries in the Spanish Caribbean have a dual identity as both Caribbean and Latin American. Some scholars even include Haiti within the Spanish Caribbean because of the shared histories of political dictatorship and frequent U.S. intervention. Unlike most areas in the British and French Caribbean, where the African influence is strongest, two of the largest islands in the Spanish Caribbean, Cuba and Puerto Rico, are made-up of 70 percent white European descendants.

Cuba

The major immigrant groups to Cuba include the Spanish, Africans, Chinese, and people from the Yucatan peninsula of Mexico. About two-thirds of Cuba's population is white, from Spanish descent, and Spanish is the national language. Cuba is mostly plains land suitable to the sugar and cattle industries. Much of Cuba's forests have been destroyed by the cultivation of sugarcane, coffee, and rice. Since Fidel Castro came to power, Cuba has belonged to a socialist economic body, the Council for Mutual Economic Assistance (Comecon).

Dominican Republic

The Dominican Republic is situated on the eastern two-thirds of the island of Hispaniola, which it shares with Haiti (a split made in 1795). On the north it is bordered by the Atlantic Ocean and on the south by the Caribbean Sea. Juan Pablo Duarte was the father of a rebellion in the 1830s that led to independence in 1844. The negative effects of Rafael Trujillo's regime, from 1930 to 1961, are still felt in the country. This regime caused much poverty and many deaths, especially deaths of Haitian immigrants who were targeted in racial attacks. The population is predominantly mulatto (of mixed European and African descent). The Spanish language has always been the major language spoken in this area, but now English has become more common, and Haitian immigrants have brought with them a French Creole. Unlike most Caribbean countries, the Dominican Republic produces much of its own food, as well as some for export. The quantity and quality of meat and dairy products has been improved in recent years due to the tourist industry. The United States and Venezuela provide imports to the Dominican Republic, and the United States receives most of its exports.

Puerto Rico

After the Spanish American War, Puerto Rico was made a U.S. territory by the Treaty of Paris, but it was granted more autonomy in 1952 with the creation of the commonwealth of Puerto Rico. The population is predominantly of Spanish descent and of mixed Spanish and African heritage, but a smaller percentage of the population descends from immigrants who came in the mid-nineteenth century from China, Italy, Corsica, Lebanon, Germany, Scotland, and Ireland. Other Caribbean peoples have come to settle in Puerto Rico: many Cubans moved to Puerto Rico after Fidel Castro came to power, and some people from the Dominican Republic have come to seek employment opportunities. Spanish is spoken in Puerto Rico, but many English words have been incorporated into the vocabulary.

The Dutch Caribbean

The former Dutch territories consist of the Dutch Windward Islands of Statia, Saba, and St. Maarten, and the Dutch Leeward Islands of Aruba, Bonaire, and Curacao. Curacao is the largest of these islands and has traditionally dominated political and economic decisions for the Dutch Caribbean. The Dutch emancipated the slaves in their colonies in 1863. After achieving independence from the Netherlands, these islands of the Caribbean formed a federation called the Netherlands Antilles, from which Aruba broke in 1986 because of problems with Curacao's (and also St. Maarten's) dominance in decision making for the territories. Dutch is still a language taught in these countries, but the people of Statia, Saba, and St. Maarten all speak English as a native tongue. The people of Aruba, Bonaire, and Curacao speak a Creole language combining Dutch, Portuguese, Spanish, English, and African languages called Papiamento or Papiamentu. This is a nonstandardized language that changes greatly from region to region within the Dutch Caribbean and has no set spelling system.

There are significant populations of Afro-Caribbeans in Curacao and Bonaire, while Aruba has more Amerindian- and European-descended populations, with one community of Afro-Caribbeans in the town of San Nicolas. St. Maarten is split into a French side and a Dutch side, because France and the Netherlands controlled different halves of the island as their colonies. The legend about this split, which happened in 1648, says that a Frenchman and a Dutchman started walking around the island in opposite directions and wherever they met up again was where they would draw the boundary separating the French section of the island from the Dutch section. The Frenchman got farther because he was only drinking wine, whereas the Dutchman did not get as far because he was drinking gin. Thus, the French received the larger portion of the island. On St. Martin/St. Maarten there are a number of languages spoken by the different groups that make up its population: French and Dutch are spoken as the official languages of the former colonial powers; English has been spoken on the island since the beginning of the nineteenth century for trade reasons and now for tourism; immigrants from Guadeloupe and Martinique speak a French Creole, while immigrants from Haiti speak a different French Creole; representatives of the Netherlands Antilles federation speak Papiamento; and immigrants from the Dominican Republic speak Spanish.

A CARIBBEAN CULTURAL PHILOSOPHY OF FOOD

One aspect of Caribbean food that distinguishes it and that links it to its indigenous and African influences, as well as its history of slavery and indentured servitude, is the idea of "making do." Making do implies using whatever is on hand or whatever can be found and using everything that is available. It is a way of operating in the Caribbean, in particular it seems by women, that can be seen as a creative, even subversive strategy. For instance, Creole languages of the Caribbean were formed out of this same environment, a need to communicate, to survive, and the creative use of the resources on hand to do so; the products of this situation, the various Creole languages, have now become distinguishing features of Caribbean culture and are used in forms of popular culture, like music and literature, as subversive manifestations of resistance.

In one scholarly work that studies this concept as it pertains to women's culture in the Caribbean, making do is discussed as a practice of liberation and empowerment, in which women "make use of available opportunities" as well as resources, and in so doing manifest a subversive presence, especially to ideas of capitalism.[1] In practical terms, this philosophy is realized when a rind of a gourd is used as a storage container or when leftover products from food preparation are turned into dishes in their own right. A practice of beach culture in Trinidad and Tobago is also part of the philosophy of making do: hanging out on the beach and eating whatever is found or caught, or sweet-talked off someone's grill, a practice known as liming.

There are many examples of making do in Caribbean food culture, in dishes that call for whatever is on hand, as in many of the stews, or in dishes that call for parts of ingredients that might otherwise be thrown away, like meat dishes made from offal. Another example of the philosophy of making do is the use of poison extracted from the cassava to make cassareep, a liquid seasoning. Borrowed from indigenous cooking methods, the use of cassareep to cook meats is still a common practice in the Caribbean in the dish called pepperpot. The butchering of animals for food in the Caribbean also partakes in the philosophy of making do. Traditionally, village butchers, especially in rural areas, are not those who have received any formal training as a butcher, but those who happen to be in possession of a set of knives sturdy enough and sharp enough to accomplish the task. Often, neighbors begin to request butchering services from them because they may be the only person for miles around with the instruments to do the job. If they have inherited the knives from someone in their family, they may have received informal, on-the-job training as an assistant to their family member. This informal training and circulation of knowledge, as well as the catch-as-catch-can nature of the availability of the necessary tools, and the improvisational manner by which Caribbean communities designate village butchers suggests another manifestation of making do both on the part of the customers who need the butcher's services and on the part of the butcher who needs a way to earn a living or to make some extra money.

In the context of work, making do is also referred to in the Caribbean as "turnin' one's han'," and it means doing whatever is necessary in order to make a living or finding ways to make money outside of formally sanctioned career paths and structures of professional training, as in the case of the Caribbean village butcher. It could mean picking up odd jobs or starting one's own business on the side, as in the case of many street and market vendors. The practice of street or market food sales in the West Indies is called "higgling," and it has been raised to an art form in many places; the women who sell foods at markets on the streets or who walk from house to house with their wares are called "higglers." This practice dates back to slavery, when slaves were allowed to sell any excess produce from their gardens and keep the money they made from these sales.

Making do is more than economics or a labor practice— it is a way of life, a philosophy, an essential part of the Caribbean woman's experience. This culinary philosophy can be traced from the arrival of the very first inhabitants of the Caribbean, who came from regions in South America and made do by living off of the bounty of the land and water of these islands. Then, it can be followed through the ingenuity of various other immigrant groups to the Caribbean who adapted their own culinary styles and many of their own ingredients to what was available to them in their new homeland, creating the blend of flavors that we know today as Creole cooking. It may be a truly authentic attitude toward food in the Caribbean, inherited from its indigenous past.

When a famous Trinidadian descendent of the Caribs, Edith Martinez (known as Queen Edith because in the 1960s and 1970s she was the reigning member of a royal, matriarchal line of Carib descendents), was asked by a writer about her people's food, she mentioned two dishes: cassava bread and pepper pot. However, she then added: "And if we don't have pepper pot, we have whatever we can find."[2] This idea of making do with "whatever we can find" infiltrates many aspects of Caribbean culture. As a philosophy of food, it implies a close relationship to local agricultural production. After all, it is emblematic of traditional peasant culture, a culture of struggle and survival. Making do is not possible for a consumer who can find any produce available year-round in her supermarket; it is a philosophy contingent upon being able to walk out into one's backyard and pick what is available. This philosophy of food can be very liberating and inspiring for the Caribbean cook, and it can also be very healthy as it often relies on fresh food products. However, there is a darker side to this cultural practice: having to make do because of concerns of class and of the Caribbean position in the global economy, that is, having to make do because of inadequate access to food products. The economic situation of having to make do, as opposed to choosing to make do as a form of cultural expression, is a grave problem for the Caribbean that affects both the quality and diversity of the foods consumed by its poor and contributes to the malnutrition and illnesses discussed in Chapter 7.

Timeline

4000 B.C.– 500 B.C.	Hunters and gatherers from neighboring areas in the Americas who had adapted to life near tropical coastlands and waterways migrate to and inhabit some Caribbean islands. They live off of hunting wild game and gathering local vegetation until about 500 B.C. when tribal peoples in the Caribbean begin to practice formalized agriculture.
1200–1492 A.D.	Taino culture flourishes despite antagonism with the Caribs. These societies eat fresh fish and wildlife and grow crops predominantly of corn, cassava, and yams, along with some beans and squash, and a wide variety of fruit trees.
1492–1502	Beginning of the colonial period in the Caribbean, which will not end for many Caribbean territories until into the twentieth century. Spanish explorer Christopher Columbus makes several journeys to and from the Caribbean initiating cultural exchange between the Caribbean and other parts of the world. He observes several new foods found in the Caribbean: allspice, chocolate (cacao), corn (maize), chile peppers, pineapples, plantain, sweet potatoes, and tomatoes. Columbus brings sugarcane and cucumbers to the Caribbean from the Canary Islands and plants them at Santo Domingo. On Columbus's second voyage to the Caribbean he plants wheat. Its cultivation is unsuccessful throughout the Caribbean and South America.
Early 1500s	Decimation of Taino and Carib cultures and the beginning of the slave trade.

1516   Fra Tomás de Berlanga, a Spanish missionary, brings oats and
            bananas to the island of Hispaniola.

1518   As the population of natives on the island of Hispaniola de-
            creases due to conditions of slave labor on the island's 28 sugar
            plantations where they have been forced to work, Spanish mer-
            chants begin to import people from Africa and force them to
            work as slaves.

1564   Sir John Hawkins brings the sweet potato to England on one of
            his ships, which had come with supplies from the West Indies
            after dropping off slaves acquired in Africa.

1565   Carrots, planted by Spanish explorers, are found growing on
            Margarita Island off the coast of Venezuela. Gonzalo Jiminez
            de Quesada brings sweet potatoes to Spain. The Spaniards
            mistake them for a type of truffle. Spanish sailors notice that
            consumption of potatoes keeps them from developing scurvy, a
            condition brought on by an inadequate intake of vitamin C.

1627   Barbados, an island never seen by Columbus, is settled by the
            British. The further colonization of Barbados is funded by the
            sale of a sugar cargo stolen from a Portuguese ship by the British
            en route to settle the island.

1636   English settlers in Barbados have been growing cotton, ginger,
            and tobacco for export and living off subsistence crops of beans
            and plantain. In 1636, the Dutch bring sugarcane from Brazil
            to Barbados. Sugarcane quickly becomes the primary crop in
            Barbados and the rest of the Caribbean, marking the beginning
            of the Caribbean's reliance on imports for its people's own con-
            sumption.

1640   More than 20,000 people are living in the British West Indies
            and involved in the cultivation of sugar.

1641   With funding by Dutch merchants, Barbados builds the first
            sugar factory in the Caribbean.

1654   The French begin growing sugarcane in Martinique, an island
            that will eventually become one of the biggest export producers
            of sugar in the Caribbean.

            Portugal ousts the Dutch from the Northeast sugar-producing
            territory of Brazil and the Dutch subsequently focus their ef-
            forts on sugar production in the Caribbean.

1655   British forces take the island of Jamaica from Spain, causing a
            three-year war between the two European powers. British con-
            trol of Jamaica means that England has its own supply of sugar,

molasses, and cacao. Britain begins giving rations of rum to its naval forces instead of beer because rum does not spoil during long sea voyages.

1660   The French begin to grow cacao beans on Martinique, but it will take another decade before Paris is supplied with cacao beans from the island.

1668   British Parliament officially invites British merchants to become involved in the slave trade, which operates in a triangular trajectory between England, Africa, and the Americas. In England, they pick up rum to give to slave traders in Africa in exchange for slaves. The slaves they acquire in Africa will be sold and they will pick up sugar and molasses in the Americas to take back to England.

1741   New England begins shipping apples to the Caribbean. Fruit like apples, which cannot successfully grow in the Caribbean climate, will become popular specialty purchase items by Caribbean consumers, especially around holidays.

1764   To protect its interest and the profits made from sales of sugar, British Parliament institutes The Sugar Act, which amends the Molasses Act of 1733 by reducing the tax on sugar brought to British colonies from colonies of other European powers. However, the British now encourage strict enforcement of this tax and staff American colonies with customs officials in order to do so.

1793   British Captain William Bligh brings breadfruit and ackee to Jamaica and St. Vincent. Both foods become essential elements in West Indian cuisine.

1804   France loses control of the western part of the island of Hispaniola after a revolution led by slaves and former slaves; subsequently, the republic of Haiti is formed. Its sugar production decreases by more than half. By the 1830s, with the end of slavery, the sugar industry in Haiti is almost nonexistent. By the 1860s, sugar production in Jamaica and in the Dutch Caribbean meets with the same fate. By the end of the nineteenth century, slaves are emancipated in almost all Caribbean territories.

1870   At the same time that slavery is abolished in the Spanish Caribbean, Caribbean islands begin exporting large quantities of bananas to North America. The exportation of coconuts is deemed unfeasible because the fruit does not sell at a profit to North American markets. Although some Caribbean regions need to find alternative export products because of the decline of the sugar industry, Cuba remains (from the 1870s to the early 1900s) a strong sugar producer with financial backing from U.S., British, and French sources.

Early 1900s   After the emancipation of many slaves throughout the late 1800s, indentured servants are brought from China, Portugal, and India to labor on the plantations. Each immigrant group brings its own distinctive culinary contributions to Caribbean food culture. Once the plantation owners can no longer find cheap labor, the plantation system crumbles and the sugar industry collapses.

1920s–   As world economies reel from the effects of the World War,
mid-1930s   sugar prices fall. By 1933, there is widespread poverty in the Caribbean, especially Puerto Rico, as a result of the collapse of the sugar industry there due to the decrease in the cost of sugar and hence a decrease in jobs and wages.

1955   Prices of many food items grown in the West Indies soar as Hurricane Janet destroys crops. Nutmeg trees in Grenada are affected, and most of the crop is wiped out.

1960s–1970s   In part because the sugar trade is no longer profitable, European colonial powers relinquish their control over many territories in the Caribbean, creating many free and independent countries.

1980s–1990s   Independent Caribbean countries begin to develop a tourist industry, which becomes their main source of revenue. American fast-food companies begin opening up chain restaurants in the Caribbean.

1994   After the fall of the Soviet Union, many Cubans attempt to flee their communist homeland in homemade boats because of food shortages caused, in part, by a U.S. trade embargo policy on Cuba. Cuba's climate makes it impossible to produce many staple food items.

2004   Caribbean food culture in the twenty-first century is affected by trends away from traditional ways of life and traditional agricultural practices. As demographics change and as infrastructure is built around the tourist economy, more islanders eat outside of the home, consumption of fast food is increasing, and fewer consumers frequent farmers' markets, while more supermarkets are being built to accommodate the increased demand. Environmentalists remain concerned with the effects of industrial development on island plant and animal life.

1

Historical Overview

THE CRADLE OF THE AMERICAS

Food in the Caribbean encompasses both the best and worst of the Caribbean's history. To speak of the Caribbean islands as a whole, as when speaking of its food culture, is to celebrate the positive: the shared cultural heritage that has come to exist among diverse groups of people, made distinct by different forms of religion, different languages, and different governmental systems. It is also to celebrate the rich ethnic and racial heritages that have blended together to create Caribbean food, and the ways in which different groups of immigrants have found peace with each other while still maintaining their cultural identities and ties to their homelands. On the other hand, many food items and cooking techniques owe their appearance in the Caribbean to the negative aspects of its history: the violence of European exploration and settlement of the Americas, the transportation of slaves from Africa, and the indentured servitude of other immigrants in the plantation system. In some cases, then, the appearance of the diverse groups of immigrants in the Caribbean who have contributed to Caribbean cuisine is due to destructive acts of colonialism. These are certainly darker moments in the history of the Caribbean, but equally important to understanding its food culture, as these historical events represent perhaps the most important patterns of migration to affect the early food history of the entire Americas.

The first island in the Caribbean to be settled by European explorers in their voyages throughout the Americas was Hispaniola, an island that is today shared by two countries: Haiti and the Dominican Republic. Christopher Columbus landed on this island in his quest for a trade route to Asia. His exploration of this island precipitated European exploration of the rest of the Americas, and thus, marked by this historical distinction, the Dominican Republic is considered the Americas' birthplace and dubbed the "Cradle of the Americas." In a similar sense, the term "Cradle of the Americas" can be used to understand food culture of the Caribbean: the foodways that have formed around the Caribbean and that have come to impact the eating habits of the Caribbean peoples are the symbolic birth of the foodways of the rest of the Americas, which also drastically changed the foodways of the entire world (among many other contributions, bringing the tomato to the Italians and the potato to the Irish). The beginning of Caribbean food culture represents the birth of the food culture of the Americas—out of this beginning has grown the shared history from which food practices in North and South America have been forged, as well as the shared conditions and patterns that continue to impact the food culture of all regions of the Americas. The results of this history include: the indigenous foods and agricultural practices of the Amerindians; the migration of food-related plant and animal life to the Americas from around the world; the imported food culture of colonizers, settlers, and immigrants who have come to the Americas; the intricacies of defining an independent national food culture; the eventual (and ongoing) loss of traditional agricultural systems; the trade issues sparked by globalization; and the health crises prompted by the growing fast food industry. All of these common Caribbean issues serve as markers of major historical periods in the history of food culture of the Americas.

INDIGENOUS AGRICULTURE

The first humans to have settled in the Caribbean came in about 4000 B.C. Although archaeologists have found the remnants of stone tools used by these people in Cuba, Haiti, and the Dominican Republic, scholars disagree as to whether or not this was the work of an indigenous group (called many names by different scholars: the Ciboney or Siboney, the Guanahatabeys, or the Barrenoid or Mordanoid societies) who are generally believed to have migrated from the area of the Bahamas by way of Florida. Archaeological evidence has been used to support the argument that these earliest people were indeed the Ciboney from the North American mainland, but the evidence also shows similarities between these people and people living on the Yucatan Peninsula of Mexico at the same time, suggesting they could have been immigrants from South America instead.

Despite the archaeological evidence supporting the idea that the earliest Caribbean peoples may have been from the North American mainland, many more Caribbean Amerindian peoples originated from South America. At one time, some of the islands in the Caribbean were geographically part of mainland Latin America; for instance, southern Trinidad was actually connected to Venezuela, according to geologists, until plate shifting and other geological events caused it to break away. Even more importantly, there seems to have been almost constant contact between the peoples on the islands and those on the mainland until at least about 600 A.D., if not continually until the time of European exploration. Despite this contact with related peoples in mainland South America, the island societies developed their own distinct culture apart from both North and South American mainlands.

By around 2000 B.C., early societies had begun to inhabit the island of Puerto Rico, as well as the islands of the Lesser Antilles (although some scholars assert that it was the immigrants from South America who began inhabiting the Lesser Antilles at this time). These early Caribbean people were predominantly a hunting and gathering society, who also fished, but there is no evidence to suggest that they developed any settled agriculture. Until about 500 B.C., they lived solely off wild game, natural vegetation, and the fish and shellfish found in their waters.

A new group of people came into the Caribbean territory in about 500 B.C., a group of farmers migrating from South America. Unlike the indigenous people already living in the Caribbean, this new group of people produced pottery and had very different customs and practices. They also lived in settlements, instead of practicing seasonal migration, and planted and cultivated food crops like manioc, as indigenous groups in South America had been doing for about a century. These people, who spoke an early Tainoan language and who are the ancestors of the modern-day Caribbean Tainos, have come to be known by the name Saladoid, a term that designates their style of pottery and that distinguishes them from the people living in the Caribbean area before them who produced no pottery, known as Aceramic people. The Saladoid people used their pottery technique to make useful materials for everyday life, especially for food cultivation and preparation. Their culture changed as it adapted itself to the

Caribbean island context and intermingled with other groups. By about 400 B.C., they had developed a slash-and-burn method of agriculture. Because agricultural deforestation requires people to move to new land after a number of years, this repeated migration and their growing numbers prompted settlements extending to the areas of Jamaica, Cuba, the Bahamas, and the entire island of Hispaniola. By about 100 to 200 A.D., as this society began to explore smaller islands, slash-and-burn agriculture was diminishing in use because it was best suited to larger territories.

The next group of people with a distinctive pottery style are known as the Ostionoids (approximately 600 to 1200 A.D.). Because the culture of the Ostionoids contained influences from both the Aceramic and Saladoid peoples, scholars believe there was a mixing of cultures that occurred over the course of generations prior to 600 A.D. However, whether this cultural interaction was a felicitous one, or whether the Aceramic peoples were colonized by the Saladoids, remains undetermined. The Ostionoid people are important because they developed the agricultural system of *conucos* (mound farming), which the people in the Caribbean were using at the time of contact with the Europeans. To make the mounded heaps into which they planted seeds, these people created nitrogen-rich soil by the method that has come to be known as composting (the mixing of decomposed organic items with soil).

The next group identifiable to archaeologists by developments in their pottery style was the Taino group, which was encountered by Europeans when they first came to the Caribbean. The Tainos are a subset in the larger Taino linguistic group of Amerindians. They were antagonized by a fierce group of Amerindians known as the Carib (from whom the name Caribbean is derived), who probably also came to the Caribbean from the Orinoco river valley in South America. The term Carib designates a linguistic group (the Cariban language) and not a tribe, but it is the word used by European explorers to identify the non-Taino group. Taino culture flourished from about 1200 to 1492 A.D., and the Taino people were extremely productive in many areas, including agriculture.

The Taino diet was very similar to the diet of people living in South America at the same time, with the exception of the variety in indigenous vegetation and game and with the exception of corn: the Taino did not process corn to make tortillas, the round, flat bread that was the staple of the Amerindian diet in many areas of South America (although they would make similar flat breads from cassava flour) but instead consumed the corn cob either raw or cooked. The Taino people frequently seasoned their food with chili peppers and ate boiled foods more often than fried.

On special occasions, they consumed beverages made from fermented corn, and European explorers made note of their custom of ritual fasting. Utensils necessary for food preparation in a Taino household included pots and jars made out of clay, strainers made from straw or wood, graters made from wood or stone, and mortars, pestles, grindstones, and mills made from stone.

The two groups of indigenous peoples residing in the Caribbean area at the time of European discovery, the Tainos and the Caribs, had no written language and thus left no recorded documents describing their civilizations. Consequently, knowledge of them can only be acquired through the accounts given by European explorers and missionaries who recorded some of the indigenous practices but who often misinterpreted them through linguistic misunderstanding or through cultural biases. This situation of European documentation of indigenous culture is further complicated by the fact that the native Caribbean peoples were wiped out so rapidly under European rule that the full intricacies of their culture could not be recorded, and many details of their culture have been lost to history.

As European colonizers explored the Caribbean islands, they encountered both the Tainos and the Caribs. The Tainos lived on the islands that are now known as the Bahamas, the Greater Antilles, and Trinidad, while the Caribs were settled in the eastern Caribbean (primarily the Virgin Islands and the Lesser Antilles). The subsequent violent encounters between European forces and the indigenous peoples, ending in their enslavement by the European colonizers, decimated their populations. The crowded conditions of their forced labor in mines and their exposure to European diseases were factors in the near genocide of these tribes, but food also played a role. Like the contemporary Caribbean peoples, the Tainos and the Caribs relied heavily on the sea as their source of dietary protein. Moved inland to mine for gold and other precious metals, both groups suffered from diseases caused by malnutrition. A diet of starches and sugars from their main crops of cassava, yam, and corn, without the protein provided by their fishing activities, proved as detrimental to these cultures as the conditions of their forced labor and exposure to European diseases. By 1550, European settlers had virtually caused the extinction of the Tainos in the Caribbean.

Based on what can be gleaned from historical and literary accounts of the early European explorers, it seems that prior to the encounter with the Europeans, the Tainos and Caribs had developed a rather rich food culture. The Taino method of planting root crops involved the use of mounded fields called *conucos*, briefly described previously, sometimes including systems of irrigation, as well as terraced farming. To plant root crops in these fields, indigenous farmers first set fire to the brush in the area to create more fertile soil, then they scooped the soil into little hills. The women then used a type of hoe called a *coa* to place cuttings from the plants into the earth. The use of this tool was described by Bartolomé de Las Casas, a Spanish missionary who traveled to the Caribbean in the early 1500s and who became an activist for indigenous rights. In *Apologética Historia Sumaria*, Las Casas wrote about how he was impressed with the area's "rich lands" that were "so fertile that with a strong fire-hardened stick they could easily dig and break the ground and prepare their fields."[1] *Conuco* farming is actually still practiced today in the Caribbean by farmers in mountainous regions of the Lesser and Greater Antilles, especially in Haiti and the Dominican Republic.

The Tainos' primary crops were squash, sweet potatoes, and other tubers, which had been brought from areas in South America to the Caribbean by their ancestors. However, the major food staple of the Taino diet was cassava (also known as manioc). So important was it to the Tainos that they instituted special religious practices dealing with the cultivation and harvesting of cassava. Cassava had been used to make the popular cassava bread in the Caribbean since about 2000 B.C. To make cassava bread, first the cassava root was ground into pulp on a type of hand-held grinder (a piece of wood with shells attached to make a rough, scraping surface), then it was strained through a type of wicker sieve to extract the poisonous liquid. Finally, it was cooked on the clay griddle known as a *buren*. There were many different types and consistencies of cassava bread, and there continues to be a great variation in recipes even today.

The Taino *conuco* system of agriculture was very well suited to the Caribbean environment as it provided good drainage and tended to prevent erosion.[2] Because it allowed for soil aeration, it was well suited to mass cultivation of the cassava, whose roots require soil with high oxygen and nitrogen levels. The usefulness of this method is noted by many agricultural historians; one writes that it "would have been a competent agricultural system without yucca [otherwise known as cassava]. With this great staple it was productive as were few parts of the world."[3] Other crops grown in *conucos* were arrowroot, peanuts, peppers, and gourds. European explorers thought this method of farming primitive and disorganized, but in reality it was a successful method of dealing with the Caribbean soil conditions and climate, and it is similar to methods of farming practiced in other tropical areas. Seed planting in gardens was also practiced by the Taino and Carib and included tobacco, corn, beans, and squash.

The food culture of the Tainos was rich because of the abundance of the land they lived on. Fruit was a large part of their diet; they regularly ate guava, custard apple, hog plum, mamey, papaya, and pineapple. They also hunted wild game for meat; some of their regular meat sources were birds, small rodents, manatees, and reptiles. From the sea, they captured conch, oysters, crabs, and other shellfish; and they practiced both saltwater and freshwater fishing. Taino society almost resembled a European feudal system in that there were two distinct classes: an upper class and a working class. The people of the working class were the ones who did the manual labor involved with the production of food for both themselves and the upper class. Archaeologists speculate that this working class was actually the remnants of a tribe conquered by the Tainos.

Tasks related to everyday life in Taino society were also divided by gender. Men did the work that prepared the fields for tending (clearing and planting), but women actually tended the crops once planted. It was the job of the children to keep birds away from the planted crops. Everybody worked together during harvest time. Generally, men fished and hunted, while women made the meals, got the water, and took care of domesticated animals like dogs and small birds.

Once self-sufficient subsistence farmers, the indigenous people's food production system was almost destroyed by the European colonial forces. However, something of their legacy has survived. For instance, many indigenous food names have survived into current usage. Historian Samuel Wilson views the sixteenth century as an overlap period, in which practices of indigenous food production influenced the European settlers and new immigrants: "the subsistence economy that developed in the sixteenth century, based on the sea's resources and heavily intercropped kitchen gardens, clearly comes in large part from preconquest, aboriginal economic practices."[4] Wilson also mentions that later immigrant groups in the Caribbean adopted surviving indigenous practices in their cultivation of manioc, sweet potatoes, yams, several varieties of beans, peanuts, peppers, sweetsop, soursop, guava, and mamey apples. The agricultural overlap period between indigenous practices and the practices of the immigrant groups to the Caribbean also contributed to the survival of indigenous knowledge of medicinal herbs and plants, fish poisons, and the fashioning of tools from natural materials.[5] More importantly, Wilson argues that the relationship of the indigenous peoples to the land, one in which they viewed themselves working peaceably and intimately with its resources, was adopted by the immigrants and thus survived to influence later Caribbean agricultural practices.[6] Besides influencing agricultural practices, indigenous methods of catching fish and seafood were also learned by European settlers and helped them to survive; these methods continue to influence current fishing practices in the Caribbean.

FISHING: FROM INDIGENOUS TIMES TO THE PRESENT

A heavy reliance on fish and seafood has characterized Caribbean food culture from indigenous times to the present. Archaeological digs in the coastlands of the Caribbean suggest that the Taino peoples relied heavily upon crab, lobster, and other shellfish in their day-to-day diets. Their favorite types of fish were barracuda, grouper, grunt, jack, parrotfish, and snapper. Indigenous people in the Caribbean fished using lines and hooks made from stone, shell, wood, and bone, and they even used sinkers made from notched stones. Indigenous fishing practices included many different techniques: night fishing by torchlight (the light would attract the fish), catching fish by hand, and sight fishing (casting the line near visible fish) in clear, shallow water with only a rod, line, and hook (this method of fishing is still practiced by some islanders who even use the traditional bamboo rods). They also used fishing tools like nets and traps. Their nets were made from a grass-like herb, whose stalks resembled rope. Stones were attached to the nets to cause them to sink into the water to catch fish.

To facilitate their fishing and interisland travel, they developed the canoe. The word canoe comes from the Carib language and actually refers to any type of boat, although today it has come to mean specifically a flat-bottomed boat made from a hollowed out, single piece of wood. The Caribs had a specific word for this type of boat in their language, from which the Spanish derived the word *piraguas* (in French, *pirogue*).

Besides using nets and traps, the indigenous people of the Caribbean used bows and arrows to catch fish (a method of fishing still popular today, known as bowfishing) and also adapted their hunting spears to the water. It is from them that the word "harpoon" entered the English language. The first harpoons were made from bone with hooks carved into the ends. Once iron was introduced by Europeans, the end of the harpoon was given a metal spike. The Tainos developed another style of harpoon, with a rod made out of wood and an attached hook at the end made out of bone or conch shell. They attached the harpoon to their ankles or wrists with a line in order to more easily pull in their catch. In most islands now, spearfishing is outlawed because of the damage it causes to coral reefs. Tourists who travel to the Caribbean for spearfishing in the few areas it is still allowed use oxygen tanks to dive under water and shoot spears out of automatic guns. Islanders who still practice spearfishing, however, do not use oxygen tanks or machinery.

Indigenous fishermen also used a number of different baits to attract fish. Mashing, a technique used also for sight fishing, requires the use of bait to chum the waters (that is, throwing small bait fish out onto the water as feed to lure large fish into the area); typically small fish are mashed against a rock and thrown into the water to attract larger fish who feed off them. They also used live bait to catch fish; indigenous fishermen tied cords around the tails of smaller fish and let them swim around to attract larger fish. They even used one species of fish that attached itself like a parasite to other fish using suckers; once this happened they reeled the larger fish in.

To catch fish, indigenous people of the Caribbean resorted to other techniques that do not resemble any standard modern-day recreational or commercial fishing practices. Using the barbasco plant, they made a mixture (harmless to humans) to put in the water that poisoned the fish. After their bodies floated to the surface, they would then simply collect the fish on the surface with nets. Yet another method of catching fish practiced by Caribbean indigenous people included the construction of wooden corrals in which they would trap fish and in which they would even raise them.

Fishing during the time of slavery in the Caribbean was a luxury for a plantation. There were a few plantations, however, that relegated slaves to fishing duties. This class of fisherman-slave enjoyed relatively more freedom than field hands or house servants. These slaves developed a popular method of netting fish in a large net, called seining, which is still practiced in the Caribbean. Seining relies on the participation of a large number of people. Fishermen out on boats keep a lookout for large schools of fish. When they are spotted, villagers on the shore throw out a large net, called a seine, and catch the school of fish in the net. To haul this large amount of fish in to shore, many hands are required. Islanders may even sing traditional songs as they tug on the ropes to bring in the net, just as African slaves did.

Another more modern type of fishing that relies on nets is called trawling. In this practice, weighted nets are used to catch fish and other seafood living on the bottom of the sea. For trawling, a large boat and much equipment is needed.

Cage traps, similar to the wooden traps used by the Caribs and Tainos, are still used in the Caribbean to catch fish and other edible sea creatures.

Traps today are made out of wire mesh and are designed in such a way that fish can get in but not out; sometimes they even include some bait on the inside of the cage to entice the fish to enter. When islanders catch fish using traps, which they call pots, they call it pot fishing. Many islands make their own pots out of various materials and have their own special designs. Usually, fishermen mark the spots where they have left their pots in the water with a buoy, but there are still some old-time fishermen who rely on their memory to remember the placement. The pots are left in the water for some time and then the fishermen go back, haul in the pot, and collect their catch. Caribbean fishermen typically catch grouper, red fish, and lobster this way.

From indigenous times to the present, the diet of Caribbean peoples has relied substantially on the bounty of the sea. Just like the Taino and Carib Indians who lived close to the coast because of the importance of marine protein to their diets, modern-day Caribbean people enjoy a great variety of fish and shellfish. Because of the abundance of different species of marine life and the preservation of knowledge and techniques of traditional fishing methods, the Caribbean is a popular travel destination for fishermen from around the world.

FOOD AND THE CONQUEST

The importance of the European discovery of the New World to food culture goes far beyond the search for a quicker trade route for spices. European settlement of the Caribbean forever changed the shape of agriculture in the Americas by the introduction of plants and animals from Europe to the Caribbean and vice versa. The Spanish created the initial impact as the first European colonizers in the Caribbean; they brought pigs, cats, chickens, goats, cattle, and other items from Spain to the Caribbean. Traveling in the other direction, they brought tobacco, corn, potatoes, tomatoes, red peppers, and yams from the Caribbean region to Europe and other parts of the sixteenth-century world for cultivation. The exchange of food items was not the only culinary exchange between the Europeans and the indigenous peoples of the Caribbean: the Amerindians taught the colonizers methods of cultivating crops in their tropical climate. The colonial period in the Caribbean was a great period of discovery and exchange between cultures, one that established the Caribbean's prominence in food culture, because this territory contributed food items that quickly became essential to foreign cuisines.

The period of conquest that marks the beginning of the colonial period in Caribbean history is also the beginning of the slave trade in the Ameri-

cas, which is intimately caught up with the history of agricultural production in the Caribbean, particularly the production of sugar. Sugarcane
was one of the most important plants to be introduced to the Caribbean
by Spanish explorers. Columbus brought it with him during his voyage of
1493, but it was not until a few years later that it was planted successfully
in Caribbean soil. By the early 1500s, once the indigenous population had
been depleted, people were being brought from Africa and forced into
slavery to work and cultivate sugarcane.

SUGAR

Near the middle of the seventeenth century, British entrepreneur-
farmers in Barbados decided to begin planting sugarcane instead of tobacco. This switch was motivated by the high demand for sugar in Europe,
a demand that would ensure large profits for those involved with the sugar
trade. Within a short while, because of its success, almost all of the European colonists in the Caribbean were engaged in sugarcane production.
The British farmers in Barbados, who had begun the trend and who made
Barbados the capital of the sugar industry for the first 30 years, began to
consolidate lands into large plantation estates and to solicit slave labor
from Africa. By the 1670s, other Caribbean areas, like the Leeward islands, Martinique, and Guadeloupe, finally caught up to the sugar production of Barbados.[7]

To make fortunes raising sugarcane, European farmers in the Caribbean
had to relinquish their traditional agricultural techniques and learn to
operate on the large scale required of the sugar industry at the time. Sugarcane was unlike any other crop that the English, for instance, had ever
raised, ripening over a much longer period than most crops, usually taking
approximately 16 months. It was also crucial to harvest the cane at the
right moment, as good quality sugar could only be made from perfectly
ripe cane. However, they had to act quickly because sugarcane spoiled
quickly once harvested. In raising sugarcane, the farmers' greatest chal-
lenge lay in developing the proper time schedule for farming activities
in relation to the nature of sugarcane. Since cane grows quickest during
the rainy season from June to November, most farmers planted their cane
from October to December and harvested the next year from January to
May. Because of the timing involved in processing the cane into sugar, the
farmers did not want all of their crops of sugarcane to ripen at once, so
they staggered their planting to ripen at intervals.[8]

Planting sugarcane was a labor-intensive activity. Cuttings from old
cane were individually planted upright in holes (in Barbados) or were

placed end-to-end in trenches and buried under a light layer of topsoil (in Jamaica). New sprouts would then grow out of the joints on the old cuttings. Cane crops were weeded often when young, and fertilized with a combination of manure and compost made from cane plant leaves when they were between one and two feet tall. Planters needed to keep large herds of cattle and sheep in order to supply all the manure necessary to fertilize their crops. After a few more months, the cane fields would become too dense for any further weeding or fertilizing.[9]

Sugarcane was harvested by the use of curved blades called bills. After they were cut, the outer leaves were stripped off, and the stalks of cane were tied together and taken to the mill. The roots of the cane would then produce a second, smaller harvest known as the ratoon. Planters in Barbados had stopped ratooning by the end of the seventeenth century and would simply pull up the cane roots and plant fresh after every harvest, but planters in Jamaica frequently ratooned two or three times before planting a new crop.[10]

The next step in the process of producing sugar was for the cane to be ground at the mill. Mills at this time usually comprised three rollers: one at the center that spun into a roller on each side. A trough placed under the rollers caught the juice from the crushed canes and ran it into a holding area before it would be boiled. The rollers in mills could be powered either by wind, water, or cattle, but they still only pressed half of what is extracted from canes today using electricity. Jamaicans favored water-powered mills, whereas cattle-powered ones were typically used in the rest of the Caribbean.[11]

Next, the cane juice was boiled to cause the water in it to evaporate and to turn it into sugar crystals. Boiling houses were usually located next to mills, as cane juice would begin to ferment if not boiled quickly. These houses consisted of large copper cauldrons placed over a furnace. Then the sugar was placed in earthen pots to cure. The molasses poured off during the curing process is the substance usually used to make rum.

This process of raising, cultivating, and processing sugarcane took an enormous amount of work on the part of the plantation's slaves. Slaves worked 6 days a week, for about 10 or 11 hours a day. During harvest, they may have even worked 7 days a week. They were purposefully given less food than they actually needed, so that they would be too weak to rebel against the slaveholders. Both white servants and black slaves on plantations looked forward to Saturdays because on that day they were given a small ration of rum and sugar.[12]

The dynamics of the sugar industry also helped the development of cattle ranching in the Caribbean. The introduction of cattle into the Caribbean by the Spanish spawned a successful ranching culture that flourished until about the end of the eighteenth century. Most of the land in the Greater Antilles during this time was used primarily for raising cattle. Large herds of cattle were kept on sugar plantations in order to provide fertilization for fields. However, ranching proved to be a profitable activity for the Caribbean colonies once the Portuguese established a sugar industry in Brazil and the resulting competition created a decline in Caribbean sugar production. Due to increased population and development of the Caribbean and less availability of ranching lands, coupled with changes in ranching practices worldwide, Caribbean cattle production has significantly declined from the colonial era, and ranchers are now dependent primarily on the United States for cattle feed, a need that places controls on the amount of cattle that can be produced in the Caribbean and in turn creates a reliance on foreign beef imports.

COLONIAL FOODWAYS

Agriculture was often the source of competition between European colonial powers controlling territories in the Caribbean. Britain, France, and the Netherlands all saw the potential for wealth in the trade of tropical fruits and vegetables grown in the Caribbean. European powers wanted control of these islands so that they could function as their countries' remote gardens and provide fresh, exotic produce for their tables, as well as the sugar they required for their desserts and beverages.

During this time, individual European colonial powers laid the framework for the basis of the major regional differences in Caribbean cuisine. Culinary traditions within the Caribbean, like linguistic and other cultural traditions, can easily be broken down into the major European colonial centers of power: British, Dutch, French, and Spanish. Subsequent immigrant food cultures from other parts of the world mixed with remnant indigenous elements and were added onto and synthesized with European customs. However, European and subsequent immigrant food traditions were all tempered by the natural landscape, the Caribbean climate, and indigenous foods. For instance, while the average continental British consumer had a relatively limited variety of fruits and vegetables from which to chose during the early years of the British conquest of Caribbean territories, because of the climate of the Caribbean and its lush tropical vegetation, the tables of the British who settled in the Caribbean were overflowing with many varieties of fresh produce year-round.

Many European settlers, especially those brought by motives of financial gain through the cultivation of tobacco and cotton, then sugarcane, and later cacao beans, adamantly did not want to relinquish their European food customs while living in the Caribbean. Those who came to the Caribbean hoping to strike it rich often desired to reproduce and emulate the lifestyles of the European upper classes. This being the case, the middle and lower classes from Europe who settled in the Caribbean are the ones directly responsible for the beginning of the creolization of cultures that gives Caribbean cooking its unique flavor. They were the ones who first adapted European cooking techniques and styles of food preparation to local, indigenous techniques and styles, as well as to local ingredients and to new ingredients being brought to the Caribbean from around the world. The middle and lower classes of European settlers brought with them techniques for preparing leftovers that were very conducive to the addition of whatever was on hand in the Caribbean. One of these dishes, salamongundy (also spelled salmagundy or solomon gundy), is now more popular in the Caribbean than in England. Also known as herring gundy and by other names in different regions, it is a method of getting another meal out of leftovers by adding salted meats and fish. One adaptation to European cooking methods was practiced by upper- and lower-class settlers alike: the use of rum in the preparation of meat dishes. Instead of the European wines and sherries they were used to cooking their meats in (liquids that only the rich could afford to import to the Caribbean and that even they saved for drinking instead of cooking), European settlers used the local Caribbean alcohol that was readily available to them: rum.

The British made a great impact on Caribbean food culture, perhaps because they were unwilling to adapt, at first, to their new environment. When British settlers first arrived in the Caribbean they were disappointed to find that the staple crops they had relied upon in England were not practical to grow in the tropical environment of the Caribbean. Worse yet, many of them found that they did not care for the taste of the indigenous crops grown there. Therefore, they began buying imported goods, like flour, salted beef, and salt fish, from English or Dutch traders.

When the British Caribbean colonies turned their lands into sugar plantations, the British settlers' reliance on imported goods increased as they had no land left to raise any other crops for their own consumption or for the consumption of their slaves. This importation resulted in bringing typical seventeenth-century British food customs to the Caribbean intact, because they imported all of the ingredients to make the dishes they were accustomed to at home.

At this time, the British diet consisted largely of cereals and dairy products, the upper classes being able to afford to add more meat to their diet than other classes. Although historians refer to the contents of this diet through the alliterative phrase "bread, beer, and beef," the Caribbean climate was not conducive to growing wheat.[13] Thus, it was impossible for the British to produce their beloved bread and beer.

Beef was also a problem. Livestock raised for beef in the Caribbean was less fatty, and therefore, less flavorful to the European palate. Ranchers at this time bred their cattle more for milk and for their hides than for their meat. However, the British found Caribbean pork to their liking— pigs were raised or hunted for their meat, which was then usually barbecued, as was done by the Taino Indians. The Caribbean's turkeys, ducks, and chickens also met with British approval. There were no techniques to preserve fresh meat at this time, so it was usually cooked quickly after slaughter. This meant that fresh meat was very expensive, so it was saved for special occasions. For everyday dishes, British settlers opted instead to purchase salted beef and pork from European and North American traders. The British also did not care for the taste of most of the fish available fresh from Caribbean waters; instead, they imported salt fish.[14]

The British did, on the contrary, enjoy the many varieties of fruits abundant in the Caribbean. They used them in jams, jellies, and sweetmeats. However, they did not find in them a substitute for their beloved British desserts, and there was a great demand in taverns and bakeries for the traditional British pastries and desserts.[15]

Other significant contributions to Caribbean food culture from British cuisine include recipes for puddings brought from England and adapted to local ingredients (like those made with jellies from local varieties of fruits and from rum, for instance) and recipes for pastie (or pattie), a flaky double pastry crust baked with a meat and vegetable filling. British settlers to the Caribbean in colonial times ate pasties made with venison, but now patties made from ground beef are the most popular. Variations on pasties are eaten throughout the many different regions of the Caribbean. The British also brought pickled fish with them from home and found that it was a cheap and easy way to feed the slaves they were bringing from Africa. However, the Africans were not accustomed to the bland cuisine of the British, and soon recipes for preparing pickled fish adapted Caribbean ingredients to create a taste appealing to the African slaves. This manner of preparing pickled fish and meats is called sousing and uses New World spices such as hot peppers, bay leaves, cloves, and black pepper to season the fish or meat.

The Scottish people, many of whom came to the Caribbean after being exiled as a consequence of the Monmouth rebellion (1685), also left their mark on Caribbean food culture. Although the diet of Scotland was similar in many respects to that of England, these Scots brought with them favorite family recipes for the traditional Scottish dish haggis, a dish of sausage made from boiled organ meats and oats accompanied by mashed potatoes and mashed turnips. In the Caribbean version of this dish, known as jug-jug, the oats are replaced by cornmeal and the mixture is not made into a sausage but served as a one-pot meal; it is particularly popular in Barbados around the Christmas holidays.[16]

So many African people were brought to the Caribbean as slaves that their population quickly became the majority during the height of the slave trade in colonial times. It is not surprising, then, that their methods of agriculture, animal husbandry, and food preparation, as well as their culinary traditions, such as specific combinations of food items, heavily influenced the nature of Caribbean cuisine. For instance, West Africans brought with them their staple dish of rice and beans, to which they imparted flavor by adding small pieces of fish or meat. Some varieties of beans, most importantly black-eyed peas, actually came from Africa, accompanying the African people on their journey from their homelands into slavery, to be used in their cooking and in others' cooking throughout the Caribbean. The combination of beans used in the staple West African dish varied by region in ingredients as well as name: Trinidadians refer to pigeon peas as congo or goongoo peas, and Jamaicans use red kidney beans in their favorite rice and bean dish called rice and peas. The flavor of the dish also varies by region: whereas the standard West African dish was flavored by meat or fish (pieces or stock), Jamaicans use coconut milk for a unique flavor.

African culture influenced not only methods of cooking and preparing foods, but agricultural practices as well. African workers established a gendered division of labor based on the cultural values of their homelands in Africa, which maintained a long-lasting influence on labor patterns in the Caribbean. African men were used to clearing the land and preparing the plot of land for planting, and they were used to working together side by side with the women to plant the crops. The women, then, were accustomed to being solely responsible for doing the weeding and tending the crops once they were planted. It just so happens that this division of labor it followed very closely the division of labor practiced by the first Amerindian farmers in the Caribbean.[17]

The African laborers who were brought to the Caribbean enjoyed making one-pot meals, a practice also very similar to the customs of the indigenous Caribbean peoples. However, although the one-pot meal in the form of stews and soups was frequent in their native homelands in Africa, preparing the one-pot meal in the Caribbean became a necessity due to the conditions of working under slavery. One of their favorite one-pot meals still enjoyed today was metagee, a stew of vegetables, coconut milk, salted meats, and hot peppers. This dish is indicative of African cooking, which is frequently both salty and spicy, and which, in the cuisine of many regions of the continent, had been incorporating the coconut for centuries before encountering it in the Americas.[18]

African food culture lent another significant feature to Caribbean food culture through the practices of the slaves. Their technique of caramelization has affected the preparation of many Caribbean foods, including desserts and especially meat dishes and was a precursor to other styles of caramelization brought to the Caribbean from Indian and Chinese cooking. The preparation of meat by caramelization in sugar creates a tangy, sweet flavor in a meat dish; the meat is fried in a caramelized mixture of coconut oil and brown sugar before it is stewed in spices and vegetables.[19]

Africans brought to the Caribbean found familiar food items like beans, cassava, and plantain; they also found that the three major staple food items they had relied on in Africa—yam, plantain, and corn—were what nourished them in the Caribbean as well. The yam, indigenous to West Africa, came with slaves in the 1670s as they were being brought to the Caribbean from Africa. The name yam comes from an African word meaning "to eat." African peoples had developed special religious observances around its cultivation, as the indigenous peoples of the Caribbean had done around the cultivation of cassava. Plantain and corn came to the Caribbean through the shipping routes of the slave trade. Plantain came to the West Indies through West Africa, where it had been brought from southern India. Corn was probably the last of these food items to arrive in Africa, but it was in use there by the beginning of the slave trade in the fifteenth century. Under slavery, corn proved to be a cheap, nutritious way to feed many people. The dish cou-cou, for instance, was a dish frequently consumed by slaves, as it was simply cooked cornmeal with okra added to it. Africans in the New World were exposed to European or Amerindian culinary methods, which they sometimes rejected. One example of this is the preparation of cornmeal porridge or gruel. Africans did not find this dish suitable to their tastes and instead preferred to prepare ears of corn by roasting them over coals. In contrast, according to the British agricultural system, corn cobs were fed to cattle, so it would have been considered by the British unfit for human consumption in that state. Instead, the slaves devised a way of baking or steaming a cornmeal mixture in banana leaves; by eating the food out of the banana leaf they dispensed with the need for a plate and utensil.[20]

Yet another familiar food Africans found in the New World was peanuts, known to them as earthnuts or ground nuts, and which was becoming one of their major crops at the time of the slave trade to the Americas. This food item was known to the West Indies during pre-Columbian times and had been taken to Africa by the Portuguese. African cuisine is highly regarded for its peanut stew bases.[21]

After the emancipation of slaves, from about 1850 to 1880, Portuguese immigrants were brought from Madeira to the Caribbean to work in the cane fields and on the sugar plantations. Most of the Portuguese immigrants settled in Trinidad and Guyana, but some went to Grenada and Jamaica as well. Madeiran cuisine was distinct from most other Portuguese cooking, which was much more strictly Mediterranean—it relied heavily on the fish and seafood of the Atlantic Ocean and consequently was well suited to the Caribbean. Also, because this cuisine had already been influenced by African traditions due to the travels of Portuguese navigators, it was easily assimilated into the African contribution to the fusion of culinary traditions happening at the time in the Caribbean. The Portuguese immigrants to the Caribbean prepared dishes that were the same or very similar to those made by Africans. For instance, they made kebabs like those found in North African cuisine, as well as the cornmeal cou-cou. However, instead of using pimento sticks to thread their meat in making the kebabs, the Madeirans used green laurel; and while Africans made rubs for their meat from allspice and selections of herbs, the Madeirans, inspired by the Mediterranean influence of the rest of Portugal's cuisine, marinated their meat in wine, garlic, black pepper, and olive oil. African immigrants brought with them their use of the coal pot for food preparation (especially well suited for one-pot meals), and the Portuguese brought a similar item for food preparation over an open fire, their *fogón*.[22]

Like many of the immigrants to the Caribbean, Portuguese immigrants at first lived a very frugal culinary existence. For breakfast, they had milho frito, a paste made from flour, water, and lard that had been left to harden and then was fried in olive oil, similar to the Italian dish polenta. One of the very cheap food sources being eaten in the Caribbean that the Portuguese were very fond of was bacalao, salt cod, a winter staple in the Portuguese diet.[23]

Salt cod was a part of the everyday diet for workers on the sugar plantations, and later, as cocoa replaced sugar as the major export product of the Caribbean, on the cocoa estates as well. Often, workers stopped only briefly to consume meals, and salt cod was frequently grilled over coals just as it was without being soaked in water. This manner of preparing the fish left it very salty, but essential minerals like sodium were required by these workers because of the amount of electrolytes lost through their sweat during work in the fields under the hot, Caribbean sun. Portuguese workers ate grilled salt cod with unleavened bread, a traditional baked good that accompanies many Portuguese meals.

As the Portuguese diet already had African influences in it, the two cuisines lent themselves to fusion. For instance, Portuguese and African flavors are brought together in the soup called callaloo, a very popular dish that has come to epitomize Caribbean cuisine, whose main ingredients are callaloo (dasheen leaves), okra, and salt cod. The salt cod (bacalao) was beloved by the Portuguese and a familiar food from their homeland, and Africans brought callaloo and okra with them to the Caribbean.[24]

Portuguese cooks were adept at handling fish and seafood and brought to the Caribbean their preparation methods. Besides bacalao, the Portuguese found many other food items in the waters of the Caribbean in order to make traditional dishes from home. Their crab dishes, especially, made a significant impact on other groups in the Caribbean. However, perhaps their greatest contribution to Caribbean fish preparation was in bringing Portuguese flavors to tuna preparation. They marinated tuna steaks in a paste that included the traditional Caribbean ingredient for fish marinade, lime juice, but that added Mediterranean flavors: red wine vinegar, olive oil, ginger, black pepper, garlic, onions, and cilantro. After thus marinating the tuna, they would barbecue it over hot coals.[25]

The two cultures had further culinary exchanges as they lived together in the Caribbean. Africans had developed a technique of cooking the meat of wild game in rum to soften it; this method is perhaps an adaptation of their use of sugar in the cooking of meats. The Portuguese also learned to prepare the meat of wild game in alcohol. However, they opted to use red wine, which was a technique of meat preparation familiar to them, and which was now possible in the Caribbean because wine was more readily available as shipments were more regular between Europe and the Caribbean. The culinary legacy left to Caribbean cooking as these Portuguese and African traditions blended is found in the contemporary preparation of meat, which usually involves both rum and wine. For instance, rabbit is most popularly prepared by first being marinating in white rum, before cooking, and then stewed in white wine during cooking.[26]

A notable absence from the Portuguese diet in the Caribbean was their baked goods and sweets. Caribbean pastries do not show any significant influence from Portuguese confectionery. Portuguese immigrants who came to the Caribbean spent their days in hard labor and rarely had the time or money for the preparation of luxury food items like desserts.[27]

Coming from a very Catholic country, the Christmas season was celebrated by these Portuguese immigrants with the preparation of traditional holiday meals. They would prepare Portuguese specialties like fried eggplant (marinated in lime juice and fried in olive oil), chilled seafood served in a spicy tomato sauce, and garlic pork. Garlic pork (also known as pickled pork) is still prepared in areas where Portuguese immigrants settled. The pork is cut into pieces, marinated in a spicy, seasoned garlic and vinegar dressing, parboiled, and finally fried.[28]

Just after the beginning of the wave of immigration of indentured servants from Portugal, Chinese indentured servants also began immigrating to the Caribbean. Most of them were brought to Trinidad and Guyana, which had started sugar cultivation later than most Caribbean countries and which still needed cheap labor in order to operate their sugar plantations after the emancipation of the slaves, but a few of them also settled in Jamaica. These Chinese immigrants were from the southern provinces of China, Fukien, and Kwangtung, where families were starving and suffering from the trade war they had lost with the United Kingdom (the First Opium War from 1839 and 1842). Because of socioreligious customs and values, women rarely left China, so there was a disproportionate number of men who immigrated from China compared to the women. Thus, Chinese men who settled in the Caribbean often cooked for themselves. Kitchens in their homes were often simple and small, frequently containing only the very necessary utensils: a wood cutting board, a wok, a cleaver, and a spatula. Initially, the traditional ingredients necessary for the preparation of their native dishes were not available. However, within a few years, toward the beginning of the twentieth century, they were able to obtain soy sauce, dried noodles, and five-star powder (a mixture of spices like cinnamon, cassia, anise, ginger, and cloves that may also include fennel and black pepper) in the Caribbean. In the first few years of Chinese immigration, even rice may not have been available to them, so homemade noodles became the base of Chinese cooking in the Caribbean. Some of the ingredients used in the cooking of southern China would have only become available recently in the twentieth century. Because they were missing the necessary ingredients to prepare traditional Chinese dishes, they did not make as significant an impact on Caribbean cuisine.[29]

The standard Chinese dish in the Caribbean today is chow mein, which consists of noodles cooked with shredded chicken in stock. More recently, small pork dumplings, known as pow, are becoming familiar to the Caribbean, but this is a later Chinese influence and does not come from the immigration of the indentured servants from China in the late 1800s. The pork required to make this dish would not have been readily available (and therefore too expensive) for the initial wave of Chinese immigrants to the Caribbean. In fact, immigrants like the Chinese who came to the Caribbean as indentured servants did not even begin to raise livestock until they were released from their indentured servant contracts and had begun their own settlements. It took until the beginning of the twentieth century for most Chinese immigrants to begin raising livestock like cattle and pigs for personal consumption. Once a steady supply of meat was available to them, the Chinese began cooking meats using their preferred method of first roasting, and then steaming them.[30]

Although other immigrant groups to the Caribbean were rather open to cultural exchange, the Chinese were less so, and they often isolated themselves from these other cultural groups. For instance, the Chinese immigrants living in the Caribbean did not adapt their diets to the readily available supply of coconut milk found in the Caribbean, as most other groups did. However, there were two aspects of life in the Caribbean that they did embrace: using rum as a marinade for meats and seafood and using the African coal pot for food preparation over charcoals.[31]

Like African slaves before them, Chinese indentured servants were allowed to supplement their rations with small gardens. In these gardens, the Chinese grew the vegetables they needed for pickling in order to make their traditional dish of mixed pickled vegetables, which is now enjoyed throughout the Caribbean. One particular vegetable that grew in the Caribbean but was not made great use of until the Chinese arrived was watercress. Watercress grew in the fast-moving freshwater around sugar mills. The Chinese used it in many varieties of soups and it became their special item to bring to farmers' markets and to sell from house to house. Africans influenced by the British culinary tradition were the only other group in the Caribbean before the Chinese to use the native watercress in their cooking, but they had used it only occasionally as an accompaniment when they made the British dish black pudding and souse.[32]

One ingredient available to the Chinese immigrants during the nineteenth century that is also seen frequently in popular Chinese cooking today in the Caribbean is honey. Honey became available during the nineteenth century when estate owners learned how to keep bees. Today, honey is mixed with soy sauce to create sauces for roasted meats.[33]

The next cultural group to come to the Caribbean to fill the need for cheap labor left vacant by the emancipation of African slaves was East Indians, who immigrated mainly to Trinidad. They brought with them white humped cattle and black water buffalo, whose raising caused changes in the ecosystems where their populations were most concentrated. The introduction of these animals furthered the effects on the Caribbean landscape of the introduction of cattle by early Spanish settlers, which included the loss of forests (and endangerment of species from the loss of forest habitat) as trees were cut down to make grazing lands, soil erosion from overgrazing, and many others.[34]

Most of these immigrants from India came from the northern area of Uttar Pradash, but others were brought from Calcutta and Bombay, and some were from Madras in southern India. Along with their food customs and traditions, they brought religious-inspired rules about what foods were proper for consumption. Basically, these rules established raw foods, in their natural state, as acceptable for consumption, and, on the contrary, foods that were cut or cooked were unacceptable because they could have become polluted according to Hindu laws.[35]

Because of these issues of contamination, dishes made of earthenware could only be used once; so, instead, food was consumed off banana leaves. Hindu laws dictated proper slaughter techniques in the preparation of meat so that it would not be polluted. These religious food laws became difficult to follow in the Caribbean, and many of the societal restrictions placed on exchanges between members of different castes had to be ignored in order to survive in the Caribbean environment. For instance, in order to get around the fact that in India members of the caste known as the untouchables could not touch food that would be consumed by a member of any other caste, Indian immigrants to the Caribbean allowed untouchables to sell fish to members of other castes, but not to clean it, thereby remaining true to the philosophy behind the law regarding cutting as an act that opens up a food to contamination, but being creative enough with the social restrictions between castes to remain true to the reality of life in the Caribbean.

Of all the immigrant ethnic groups, Indians coming to the Caribbean as indentured servants did not recognize the majority of food items that they were given to eat as part of their rations. Their diet consisted mainly of staple carbohydrates and some seasonal vegetables. Most could not afford any additional supplement to their diet as they would have been charged for extra food items and their wages were almost nonexistent. Indian families could usually afford only the ingredients to make their traditional breads, chappati or roti, which required only flour and water, and which were made on a special griddle, called a *tawa*, brought by Indian immigrants to the Caribbean. However, they could not afford to make the traditional accompaniments to go with these breads, like dahl, a type of porridge made from lentils. Instead, they would eat these breads with some of the local Caribbean varieties of pepper, or wild spinach (called baji). Judging by their availability and the frequency of their consumption by many ethnic groups, chappati and roti, especially, are still some of the most popular Indian foods in the Caribbean.[36]

Indian immigrants would not have had ready access to meat as it was very expensive, but this did not matter to some of them, who followed vegetarian diets based on Hindu laws. However, in the Caribbean at this time, even rice (a staple of vegetarian and nonvegetarian Indians alike) was very expensive and at first did not constitute a regular part of their diet. Instead, making necessary changes to their traditional cuisine, they came to rely on breads as the essential carbohydrate in their diet, and they also took readily to the coconut and adapted it into their everyday diets, drinking large quantities of coconut water.[37]

The breads that replaced the missing rice in their dishes were varying combinations of the same inexpensive base: flour and water. They added some sugar and baking powder to the basic flour and water combination and achieved a dough that, when fried, was known as metai. In another fried bread, ground split peas, curry powder, and baking soda join the flour and water combination to make a dough that, when fried, is known as bara. Bara is used in one of the most popular snacks throughout the Caribbean, doubles, which requires two bara sandwiched together with some ground, curried chickpeas (channa) in the middle. These Indian immigrants also adapted the ubiquitous salt fish into their diets and combined it with their expertise for fried breads, creating the dish accra and floats, which is a dish of fried, minced salt fish balls served with a fried bread.[38]

Rich Indian families in the Caribbean might have been able to eventually keep a cow in order to have fresh milk. From the milk they would have been able to produce yoghurt and ghee (clarified butter), two essential ingredients in Indian cuisine. According to Indian food customs, any food cooked in ghee would be purified. Ghee would have been made at home at the time of these immigrants but now is available prepackaged from the store.[39]

The Indian immigrants who came to the Caribbean at this time were skilled in the cultivation of rice. It was not long before they helped Trinidad and Guyana to achieve a booming rice industry, which made rice readily available to Indian families in the Caribbean.[40]

As is obvious from the discussion of the new food items brought to the Caribbean with each different immigrant group, many foreign food items were brought during colonial times. Even the mango, whose flavor has become synonymous with Caribbean cooking, was brought from its native India by the Portuguese first to Africa and then to the New World during the sixteenth century. Although many important food items were taken from the Caribbean to other parts of the world to become distinguishing characteristics of various ethnic cuisines, European powers in the colonial era brought many trees and plants to the Caribbean that would later become distinguishing aspects of its cuisine. Some imported plants and trees did better than others; for instance the fig, the cherry, and the orange did not do well in the tropical Caribbean climate. Although agricultural specialists have developed varieties of these fruit trees that successfully grow fruit in the Caribbean, these are considered luxury or specialty items and are not a regular or essential feature of Caribbean cuisine. Some food items identified as typically Caribbean migrated with early indigenous peoples from other parts of the Americas: limes, avocados, pomegranates, lemons, and citrons were brought from mainland South America with these early settlers.

Although many of these food items became part of local island diets, the preoccupation of European powers during the colonial era was the identification of items that could be exported from the Caribbean to the rest of the world for great profit. Therefore, besides sugar and cattle, during the colonial period bananas, which had been identified as another important cash crop for the Caribbean, began to be cultivated on a large scale and were first exported in the 1860s. The first market for Caribbean bananas was the United States. Cuba and Jamaica were the first two Caribbean territories to export bananas, but many islands— Dominica, St. Lucia, St. Vincent, and Grenada—followed suit. In the 1920s, disease wiped out much of the banana crop in the Caribbean, and the industry has never fully recovered, due in part to competition from the exportation of bananas by U.S. corporations based in Latin America.

INDEPENDENCE AND AGRICULTURAL EXPORT-LED DEVELOPMENT

Food production, historically, has been a major factor of daily life in the Caribbean as the majority of its population has, traditionally, been employed in the agricultural sector. In comparison to the United States, for instance, in the 1970s when only 6 percent of the U.S. population was

Jamaican farmers planting red peas. © Art Directors and TRIP/Dave Saunders.

involved in agricultural production, 40 percent of the population in the Caribbean region was producing agriculture.[41] Recently, however, due to the politics of export-led development (an economy based on the production of agricultural items for export, which leaves a country dependent on purchasing imported food items for its own consumption) and the changes it has wrought on the cultural landscape of the Caribbean, this situation has changed. Now there are more Caribbean people employed in the tourist industry by hotel chains, resorts, and cruise liners than there are people who work the land.

The pattern of exportation and importation of foodstuffs that still plagues the Caribbean was established with early colonization. European settlers used Caribbean land to cultivate items like sugarcane for export back to Europe and relied on imports from Europe for many of their needs. Not much land was given over to production of foods for island consumption, if any, until the late colonial era when slaves were given small plots of land to grow crops for their own consumption in the small amount of time when they were not working in the fields. The pattern established in the early colonial days is still the norm today and is known as export-led development or growth.

Although steps were made after the independence of Caribbean colonies to harness the richness of Caribbean agriculture as a significant means of improving their economies, the main source of income for Caribbean territories became tourism. While the Caribbean had been a popular travel spot for the wealthier classes during the nineteenth century, by the mid-twentieth century, travel to the Caribbean had become possible for the middle classes as well. Tourism had become so popular in the Caribbean, in fact, that the number of annual visitors per year began to greatly exceed the number of residents on many islands.[42]

Culinary tourism has become one of the significant draws of tourists to the Caribbean. Reflecting this trend, the time of Caribbean independence marks the beginning of massive publications of Caribbean cookbooks.[43] These cookbooks helped to solidify national cultures within the Caribbean and also provided ways for tourists to take home more than trinkets from their Caribbean vacation, but to reproduce the culinary delights they had experienced during their trips. Caribbean nationals living abroad were also audiences for these cookbooks and found them useful in reminding them of how to prepare well-loved dishes from their homelands. Because colonial powers suppressed regional, national, and particularly indigenous cultural identities in the Caribbean, the time of independence was a time of renewed fervor for any outward cultural practices considered traditionally or authentically Caribbean.

Despite this fervor for authentic Caribbean culture, a return to a Caribbean culture predating European colonization was impossible as Caribbean culture had by now become defined by its mix of European, African, Asian, and Amerindian cultural traditions. Moreover, a return to agricultural practices that would honor traditional Caribbean lifestyles had become almost impossible. Due to decisions made during the colonial era, governmental decisions about agriculture affecting Caribbean food culture did little to stop the increasing loss of traditional methods of farming and fishing. For instance, a major cause of the export-led growth pursued by Caribbean governments after their independence from European colonial forces was the continued legacy of mono-crop production initiated by colonial forces. Since colonial times, the production of sugar for export has been the major agricultural activity in the Caribbean, with the production of bananas, cocoa, coconuts, coffee, tobacco, and citrus fruits for foreign consumption following close behind. Agricultural production for domestic consumption in the Caribbean consists mainly of corn, rice, root crops, and tropical fruits, with some scattered, local production of livestock and poultry.[44] However, even agricultural production for domestic consumption in the Caribbean is problematic given the number of local laborers needed to provide fresh produce for the dining rooms of island hotels and resorts. Because Caribbean leaders did not diversify local agricultural production, the Caribbean continues to rely heavily on other countries for the importation of its food supplies. Politically, the era of independence was not at first the great celebration of Caribbean culture that many thought it would be; instead, in an economic hierarchy, European colonizers were simply replaced by tourists. Because of this situation, it is perhaps understandable that significant numbers of Caribbean peoples have sought to leave their homelands after independence.

EMIGRATION AND PAN-CARIBBEAN FOOD CULTURE

Not only have a variety of national cultures influenced Caribbean food culture through the people that have come to live together there, but the travel of Caribbean nationals to other countries, especially after the period in which many of the countries achieved independence from European colonial countries, has helped to bring centers of Caribbean culture to other parts of the world. New York City currently has almost as great a Puerto Rican population as the Puerto Rican capital city of San Juan.[45] The same is true of New York City's Dominican population. Miami has also become a major center of Caribbean culture with immigrants from Cuba, Jamaica, Haiti, and other Caribbean countries. Other cities like London and Toronto also have large Caribbean populations.

Responding to this trend of emigration, Caribbean cookbooks began to account for a new audience: Caribbean nationals living abroad. One particular Jamaican cookbook written in 1963, just a year after Jamaica achieved its independence, addressed itself to "Jamaicans living away from home who have a nostalgic longing for dishes peculiarly Jamaican, and also to visitors to Jamaica who have a flair for cooking and would like to try their hands at the dishes they have enjoyed here."[46] These emigrants have also authored a number of cookbooks, usually with the stated purpose of retaining and sharing their cultural identity in their new environment.[47] Caribbean independence from European colonial forces initiated a celebration of Caribbean culture that was eventually felt in literature, the visual arts, music, and most importantly, food.

The period of post-independence has witnessed another transformation in the treatment of food in Caribbean cookbooks. While cookbooks published in Jamaica, for instance, published after 1970 only speak of Jamaican cuisine with no reference to the larger Caribbean as a whole, the actual content of many of these cookbooks was interchangeable with cookbooks being published at the time on Bahamian cuisine or on Caribbean cooking as a whole.[48] Many cookbooks made special note of national dishes, but overall, they acknowledged a pan-Caribbean food culture: "a common Creole Caribbean cuisine [distinguished by] spice[s], and ... seen as the product of a blending of cuisines from other places."[49] This trend in culinary thought as presented in cookbooks led many cookbooks to use the same image to symbolize this pan-Caribbean food: the image of the melting pot.[50]

Tourism, too, was a factor in creating the notion of a pan-Caribbean cuisine. Tourists who traveled to different islands wanted to find the same foods they liked at each one. In this respect, in deference to the tourist, pan-Caribbean cuisine was like the standardization in chain restaurants that Americans especially had come to expect. As a matter of fact, in the 1960s and 1970s, American fast food restaurants began competing with each other for markets within the Caribbean, with most major fast food chains opening franchises in the Caribbean around this time. At first, their main business was from the tourist industry, but because most other restaurants in the Caribbean are also directed to tourists, eventually the fast food chains in the Caribbean picked up a steady stream of Caribbean clientele as well.

The increased movement of goods, symbols, capital, and people making individual nationalities more irrelevant, a phenomenon known as globalization, has also served to temper identification of regional Caribbean cultures so that speaking of a wider Caribbean culture is no longer as problematic as it once was when individual localities differed from each other greatly. Tourism has certainly been responsible for some of this trend. While at one time the great diversity of the many islands contributed to the richness of the experience of the Caribbean, encroaching global capitalism has made for a more heterogeneous Caribbean culture in which local differences and regional specialties become harder to identify or access. In this sense, however, the Caribbean is only continuing, like many other countries in the Americas, a process starting during colonial times of embracing a greater global culture as its own.

This global trend is certainly a two-way street, as people all over the world enjoy the special blends of flavors and textures that constitute Caribbean cooking. Caribbean nationals living abroad have contributed significantly to the enjoyment of Caribbean cuisine on an international scale. Thanks to the diligence of the large communities of Caribbean peoples living together in places like New York, Boston, London, and Toronto, and to the demand from tourists who have traveled to the Caribbean and fallen in love with its culinary delights, it is not uncommon in these places to find Caribbean grocery stores and restaurants readily available, so that everyone can enjoy one of the most culturally diverse American cuisines.

NOTES

1. Bartolome De las Casas, *Apologética Historia Sumaria*, cited in Ignacio Olazagasti, "The Material Culture of the Taino Indians," in *The Indigenous People of the Caribbean*, ed. Samuel Wilson (Gainesville: University Press of Florida, 1997), p. 131.

2. Jan Rogozinski, *A Brief History of the Caribbean: From the Arawak and the Carib to the Present* (New York: Facts on File, 1992), p. 15.

3. Ibid.

4. Samuel Wilson, "Introduction," in *The Legacy of the Indigenous People of the Caribbean*, p. 208.

5. Wilson, pp. 208–9.

6. Wilson, p. 209.

7. Richard S. Dunn, *Sugar and Slaves: The Rise of the Planter Class in the English West Indies, 1624–1713* (Chapel Hill: University of North Carolina Press, 1972) pp. 19–20, 188.

8. Ibid, p. 191.

9. Ibid, p. 191.

10. Ibid, p. 192.

11. Ibid, pp. 192–94.

12. Ibid, pp. 194–95, 248.

13. Thomas Tusser, quoted in Ibid, p. 273.

14. Ibid, p. 275.

15. Ibid, p. 278.

16. Christine Mackie, *Life and Food in the Caribbean* (New York: New Amsterdam, 1991), pp. 62–63.

17. M. J. Herskovits, quoted in Ibid, p. 73.

18. Ibid, p. 73.

19. Ibid, pp. 76–77.

20. Ibid, pp. 77–81.

21. Ibid, pp. 82–83.

22. Ibid, pp. 107–13.

23. Ibid, pp. 113–17.

24. Ibid, pp. 117–18.

25. Ibid, p. 120.

26. Ibid, pp. 122–23.

27. Ibid, pp. 123–24.

28. Ibid, pp. 125–26.

29. Ibid, pp. 131–34.

30. Ibid, pp. 135–37.

31. Ibid, pp. 137–38.

32. Ibid, pp. 138–40.

33. Ibid, pp. 144–45.

34. Ibid, p. 150.

35. Ibid, p. 151.

36. Ibid, pp. 152–54.

37. Ibid, pp. 152, 157.

38. Ibid, pp. 154–55.

39. Ibid, p. 155.

40. Ibid, p. 155.

41. Wilbur F. Buck, *Agriculture and Trade of the Caribbean Region* (Washington, D.C.: U.S. Department of Agriculture Economic Research Service, 1971), p. 1.

42. John Gilmore, *Faces of the Caribbean* (London: Latin America Bureau, 2000), p. 43.

43. B. W. Higman, "Cookbooks and Caribbean Cultural Identity: An English-Language Hors D'Oeuvre," *New West Indian Guide/Nieuwe West-Indische Gids* 72, nos. 1 and 2 (1998), p. 79.

44. Buck, p. 2.

45. Richard Hillman, "Introduction," in *Understanding the Contemporary Caribbean*, ed. Richard S. Hillman and Thomas J. D'Agostino (Boulder, Colo.: Lynne Rienner, 2003), p. 2.

46. Higman, p. 83.

47. Ibid, p. 86.

48. Ibid, pp. 84–85.

49. Ibid, p. 85.

50. Ibid.

2

Major Foods and Ingredients

Because most authentic Caribbean cooking is based on the philosophy of making do discussed in the Introduction, the foods and ingredients traditionally used have been either those that thrive in the tropical climate and grow locally (whether indigenous or not) or those imported goods that have become a regular part of the Caribbean diet over time and that are readily available as part of established trade routes. Many imported foods have been brought to the Caribbean for the purpose of providing necessary ingredients in the cuisines of various immigrant groups. This mix of cultures that has come to inform the Caribbean pantry makes it one of the most diverse cuisines in the Americas; this also means that the foods available in Caribbean markets are often similar to those in markets of Latin America and Africa.

HERBS, SPICES, CONDIMENTS, SEASONINGS, AND FLAVORINGS

One of the features that distinguishes Caribbean cooking is its use of seasonings and condiments. Any true Caribbean kitchen stocks a host of preserves, chutneys, flavored rums, and fresh or dried spices to make home-mixed rubs for meats, fish, and poultry. The use of spices and seasonings in Caribbean cooking is due in large part to the prolific quantity of herbs and spices growing naturally in this tropical region.

Caribbean cooks have also learned to rely on seasonings and spices due to the rigors of proper food preparation under the tropical sun. Before refrigeration, seasonings were used to preserve foods so that they did not spoil in the Caribbean heat. Amerindians developed techniques of food preservation like smoking, and they seasoned their foods with three main ingredients: chili peppers, *cassareep* (made from cassava), and annatto. Later, their descendants and other immigrant groups turned to methods like curing, pickling, salting, and candying. Spices, seasonings, and sauces also became important to Caribbean cooking because of the poorer quality foods that immigrant groups to the Caribbean were given under slavery and indentured servitude.

Some spices and seasonings are found throughout the Caribbean in typical meals, such as allspice, nutmeg, cloves, cinnamon, and ginger. Jamaica, in particular, is known for the outstanding quality of ginger produced locally; therefore, many Jamaican recipes feature ginger flavors. However, perhaps the most important flavor that distinguishes typical meals in the Caribbean diet is the hot pepper. Many varieties are used throughout the islands. Usually, typical meals prepared with hot peppers call for the whole pepper to sit in the liquid with the ingredients while they cook.

In the English Caribbean, stews always start off with basic seasonings like scallion (green onions that are called sive), parsley or coriander leaves, and thyme. In Bajan cooking (the cooking of the island of Barbados), most recipes for poultry, meat, and seafood begin with a base called seasonin'; this is a paste made from garlic, chives, peppers, and chilies, that is not as hot as spice mixtures for jerked meats. Barbados has another special seasoning blend called chopped seasoning, which is used in the preparation of chicken, pork, and fish, especially for frying flying fish. Chopped seasoning is similar to seasonin' and is made with onion, bell pepper, chili pepper, garlic, butter, thyme, parsley, lime juice, and black pepper.

The East Indian influence in the Caribbean has contributed a variety of relishes and chutneys to accompany rice and curry dishes. Indian dishes made in the Caribbean require *masala*, a seasoning mixture made from coriander seeds, anise, cloves, cumin, fenugreek, mustard, and turmeric. Curry is known as colombo in the French Caribbean, derived from the name of the Sri Lankan city by the same name. Although curry powder has come to be known as the quintessential spice mix of Indian cooking, in the Caribbean, specifically Trinidad and Tobago, another spice mix, garam masala, is often preferred. Garam masala is used like curry powder in cooking, but it does not have the turmeric base of curry. Instead, it is a mix of coriander, anise, cloves, fennel, cumin, cardamom, sesame seeds, black pepper, cinnamon, nutmeg, and bay leaves.

Caribbean cooks now tend to purchase colombo powder commercially prepared from supermarkets instead of making their own. However, many commercially prepared spices contain high quantities of monosodium glutamate for freshness. When making spice mixes at home, it is important to use whole spices, not ground ones, as pre-ground spices do not contain the full quantity of aromatic oils necessary to making a good spice mix. Homemade spice mixes should be used sparingly in cooking as they are often much more flavorful than commercially prepared ones.

Trinidad has a special region from which it obtains most of its seasoning herbs. The hilltop town of Paramin and its surrounding countryside supply the majority of the island's herbs from its large quantities of fresh parsley, thyme, mint, chives, and culentro. This last herb is known as *chandon beni* in Trinidad, which means false cilantro, and it lends the definitive flavor to Trinidadian cooking. In Caribbean cooking, the general term used to designate freshly gathered, local herbs and spices is the word "bush" or "bush herbs," and it can mean plants gathered in the wild or grown in yards.

Cooks in the Spanish Caribbean season with *sofrito* (a sauce made from a mixture of peppers, herbs, olive oil, annatto, and sometimes tomato paste), cilantro (known as coriander leaves in the British Caribbean), green peppers, onions, garlic, and tomatoes. In Puerto Rico, main dishes are generally seasoned with either *sofrito* or *adobo* (a mixture of spices, herbs, and sometimes tomato paste). Puerto Ricans especially enjoy meats or seafood sprinkled with a basic *adobo* then pan-fried or grilled. In Cuba, however, *adobo* is not a dry or paste-like mix of spices and herbs, but instead is a popular liquid marinade for meats made from the seasoned juice of the sour orange (a variety of orange named *naranja agria*), which looks like a lumpy unripe orange but actually tastes like a lime (fresh lime juice is often used instead). The Cuban version of *adobo* is used as a marinade to make one of its renowned national dishes: *lechon asado* (roast suckling pig). Cubans also make a cooked sauce from the bitter orange, called *mojo*, that they refrigerate and then pour on many of their foods as they consume them.

English and French Caribbean cooking will only rarely use Spanish Caribbean spice mixtures in their typical dishes; when they use an annatto- (achiote-) based seasoning mix like *sofrito* in a dish, for instance, it is called *roucou*. Instead, French Caribbean soups and stews use a thickening base called a *roux* that consists of flour browned in oil, and that lends a nutty flavor to its dishes. Although recipes for seasoning mixes vary by cook, there are two main variations in recipes for the Spanish seasoning *sofrito*: red or green. Red *sofrito* is made with red bell peppers and/or tomatoes; it is most frequently found in Cuba, whereas green *sofrito*, made with green bell peppers, is more popular and is the only *sofrito* used in Puerto Rican cooking, where it is sometimes called *recaito*.

The French Caribbean uses a table sauce seasoning called *sauce chien*, meaning dog sauce, which is very spicy and made from vegetables. In the French West Indian version of this sauce, the recipe also calls for lime juice, so it is somewhat similar in taste to the Cuban *mojo*. *Sauce chien* is used as a condiment, like the hot pepper sauces in other parts of the Caribbean (such as *ajilimojili*), when eating seafood and poultry. Some say that its spiciness helps extract any toxins in the seafood that might cause allergic reactions. A similar seasoning is served with meat dishes in Haiti, particularly on pork, and is a fresh hot sauce made from chile peppers, lime juice, and onions, known as *sauce ti-malice* (see Chapter 6 for the recipe). In the Dutch Caribbean, the pepper sauce used at tables is called *pika* and is really a sauce made from finely chopped onions and chili peppers pickled in vinegar. The French Caribbean, too, has a hot, vinegar-based condiment sauce called *picklese*, not to be confused with *pikliz*, which is, more often than not, a spicy cabbage salad made with the chile pepper-soaked vinegar. Also, generally throughout the Caribbean, spicy olive oil (made by soaking chili peppers in olive oil and given extra flavor from the addition of garlic cloves, black pepper, allspice, thyme, and bay leaves), called rather bluntly fire oil, may be drizzled onto foods before consuming them. This is a legacy brought by the Portuguese, who brought piri-piri, a chili pepper-soaked olive oil to the Caribbean.

Another distinct flavor of Caribbean cooking is the simple seasoning of fish with fresh citrus juices, like lime. This flavoring and preserving technique is practiced throughout the Caribbean and Latin America in order to cut the pungent flavor of fish and seafood. Lemons and limes were brought from Spain with early explorers.

Achiote (Bixa Orellana)

Achiote is a food ingredient made from the seeds of the annatto tree and used to give a yellow or orange color to foods, including butter, margarine, cheeses, and smoked fish. In its paste form, prepared by grinding achiote seeds together with some spices, it gives a smoky flavor to meats, fish, and poultry when rubbed on as a marinade coating before cooking. It is most widely used in *sofritos* in the Spanish Caribbean and in the *blaffs* and *mignans* of the French Caribbean (where it is known as *roucou*). The seeds of the annatto tree can also be used to make an oil (annatto oil) or to make butter (annatto butter). Indigenous peoples of the Caribbean smeared achiote onto their bodies for use as an insect repellant, as did

Native Americans in U.S. territories who, because of this practice, were given the name redskins.

Achiote seeds are sold in small plastic bags in Latin American or Caribbean grocery stores. Achiote seeds should be a bright reddish color; if they have already turned brown, then they will have lost their flavor. Achiote paste can also be found prepackaged, mixed with spices and vinegar. Sometimes achiote paste will be sold in the shape of a small brick, often called *recado colorado*.

Allspice (Pimenta Dioica or Pimenta Officinalis)

Allspice comes from the berries of the evergreen pimento tree, a member of the myrtle family and native to Jamaica. In the French Caribbean it is known as *bois d'Inde* and used to season *blaffs* (poached fish dishes) and Creole blood sausage. Spanish colonizers named the spice pimento because the dried berries used in cooking looked like peppercorns (for further name confusion related to pimento see the section on chili peppers). In Jamaica, it is still known as pimento and it is the main seasoning for the popular dish Jamaican jerk. All the parts of the tree are used in cooking. For instance, true Jamaican jerk is prepared on a fire made from allspice branches, lending a particular flavor to the jerked foods. Allspice berries, known as pimento seeds, are also a popular pickling spice. This spice tastes like a blend of cinnamon, cloves, black pepper, and nutmeg.

Arrowroot (Maranta Arundinacea)

Arrowroot is a root that is dried and ground into a powder for use as a thickener. It is also known as West Indian arrowroot, Bermuda arrowroot, or St. Vincent arrowroot. The island of St. Vincent is the world's leading supplier of arrowroot. Leaves of the perennial plant are spear-shaped and the root is light gray. The name comes from the use of the plant by the indigenous peoples of the Caribbean to treat wounds inflicted by poisoned arrows. In addition to its many other uses, arrowroot is still used as an antidote to some poisons.

Chandon Beni or Shandon Beni (Eryngium Foetidum)

This herb is referred to as false cilantro because it resembles and is related to cilantro. It is also known as *recao*, long coriander, saw-tooth coriander, culantro, or shadow beni. The leaves of the culantro plant are used like cilantro but the roots are consumed in various dishes as well. Culantro is the key ingredient in the popular Puerto Rican seasoning base called *sofrito*.

Chili Peppers (Capsicum Frutens)

The history of the chili pepper in the Caribbean begins with a confusion of names. While the Indians called it *aji,* Columbus called it pepper (in Spanish, *pimiento*) because he believed the spice in his food was related to the black pepper (in Spanish, *pimienta*) he was trying to find. Black pepper (*piper nigrum*) is actually derived from a different plant. When Spanish conquistadors began exploring Central America, in the early 1500s, they learned its Nahuatl name, *chilli,* and began calling it *chile,* in Spanish (or *chili,* in English). In the indigenous diet, chilies, rich in vitamins A and C, were used in soups and stews. They are an integral ingredient, for instance, in the famous Caribbean indigenous stewed dish known as pepperpot.

Scotch bonnet peppers, closely related to habanero peppers, are perhaps the most widely used in the Caribbean and are, for many, the defining flavor of Caribbean cooking. They come in a variety of colors (green, yellow, orange, red, and white) and are extremely hot. Their name comes from their appearance: the Scotch bonnet pepper is shaped like a lantern and their crinkled tops look similar to traditional Scottish hats. Jamaicans call the Scotch bonnet pepper bonnie. Scotch bonnet peppers in the Caribbean can be bought fresh from farmers' markets in late summer and fall. Otherwise, cooks use dried chili peppers, bottled sauces, or other varieties of peppers that may have been imported.

Although the Scotch bonnet pepper is the favorite variety of pepper in most of the Caribbean, in Trinidad and Tobago the chili pepper of choice is a congo chili pepper, a pod-type pepper. Congo chilies are only available in Trinidad and Tobago. The second favorite to the Scotch bonnet pepper in Caribbean cuisine is the bird pepper, which is also extremely hot. Other chilies used in Caribbean cooking are *Bonda Man' Jacques, Piment Negresse,* and *wiri wiri.* Fresh jalapeño peppers or habanero peppers may be used as a substitute in recipes, but they are not as hot.

The use of chili peppers in traditional Caribbean cooking may be a response to the natural environment, the heat of this tropical region, as chilies, when eaten, cause the body to sweat and thus to cool itself off. Also, many people report a kind of "high" achieved by eating chili peppers, since the pain from their heat causes the body to respond by releasing endorphins, its own natural painkillers. Chili peppers also have many dietary benefits. According to some recent studies done in Japan and England, the consumption of chili peppers increases the body's metabolism and the rate at which it burns calories, and they also have antioxidant properties.

While cutting or slicing hot peppers, it is advisable to wear gloves. Chili peppers contain the chemical capsaicin (which lends them their heat), which can irritate the skin. This chemical is concentrated mainly in the seeds of the peppers, so for many recipes containing peppers, the chilies should be sliced open and the seeds removed before chopping or slicing the pepper. If a whole chili is used in a dish like a soup—where a whole chili is placed in a pot and gives the broth flavor—it should be removed from the dish before it bursts or the exposure of the dish to the hot pepper seeds may impart too much spice to it. If using a blender to grind whole dried chili peppers, it should be covered with a dish towel so as not to inhale fine dust particles from the chilies. The burning sensation in the mouth caused by chili peppers can be stopped by the consumption of a dairy product like milk or ice cream, although almost every Caribbean native has a preferred remedy to cure a chili burn.

Bottled hot pepper sauces are popular in the Caribbean, and many varieties and flavors are available. In Jamaica, the favorite brand of hot sauce is Pickapeppa, in either the red or brown variety. The Pickapeppa company was started by Norman Nash, and the sauce is produced in the Don Figuero mountains of Mandeville, Jamaica. This is perhaps one of the most well-reputed hot pepper sauces and is made from a secret recipe.

Another famous brand is Caribbean Gourmet, made from Scotch bonnet peppers. The Trinidadian company Karibbean Flavors offers hot pepper sauce with tamarind added as a flavor. The brand Matouk's makes many types of hot sauces, most of which are based on the Scotch bonnet pepper; they have a particularly popular variety that is flavored with papaya. Ocho Rios is another favorite Jamaican brand; they make various kinds of sauces ranging from spicy ketchups and mustards to red pepper sauces like tabasco. Windmill, a company from Barbados, makes a mustard-colored hot pepper sauce. A popular green pepper sauce is made by the Turban company. Some other types of world-renowned hot pepper sauces from the Caribbean include Bermudan hot pepper sherry and Trini hot pepper wine. Hot pepper sherry is even popular for use in making the alcoholic drink the Bloody Mary. Some Caribbean cooks still make their own hot sauce by soaking hot peppers in vinegar and herbs.

Chocolate (Theobroma Cacao)

Chocolate is known as cocoa or cacao in its bean form. Columbus found cocoa beans in parts of Central and South America on his second voyage and took them back to Spain. The Spanish later cultivated the cocoa tree in Trinidad beginning in the mid 1620s, and it spread to other areas in the Caribbean. Although the cocoa tree is native to South America, it now grows in many tropical climates like Africa, where it is cultivated commercially.

When the pods on the cocoa tree turn brownish-red they are ripe. After the beans are removed from the pods, they are dried in the sun before being roasted. Besides chocolate, the roasted beans are used to make commercial cocoa powder and cocoa butter.

Industrial production of chocolate as the candy known today did not begin until the mid-nineteenth century. The Caribbean cocoa industry provided a great source of income for the British during World War I. However, to help the Germans after World War II, the British drove down prices. The consequence was the ruin of many cocoa-cultivating families in the Caribbean.

Cilantro (Coriander Sativum)

Cilantro is the Spanish name for the coriander plant, the leaves of which are used as an herb in cooking. Cilantro is often used similarly to the way parsley is used in other cuisines. The herb has a cooling effect when used in spicy hot foods. Many Caribbean peoples use cilantro as a breath freshener by chewing on the leaves after eating meals that have been heavily seasoned with garlic.

Ginger (Zingiber Officinale)

The ginger plant is from the same family as turmeric and cardamom. The part of the ginger plant most used in cooking is the gingerroot, which is actually not the root but the rhizome of the perennial plant whose leaves and stalks look similar to bamboo. Jamaica is known for producing some of the world's finest ginger and has come to be called "the land of ginger." The ginger plant was brought to the Caribbean by European explorers who had gotten it from Asia. Ginger is used to make many different foods in the Caribbean, from ginger cookies and gingerbread to candied ginger, ginger beer, and ginger cider (alcoholic or nonalcoholic). Ginger is now even one of the ingredients in most jerk seasonings.

Nutmeg (Myristica Fragrans)

Nutmeg comes from a tropical evergreen tree. The tree was brought to the Caribbean (to Grenada) in 1824 from the East Indies. The part used to make a powder used in cooking is the rounded, withered-looking, brown nut. The spice mace is actually made from the red fibrous outer layer of the nut of the nutmeg tree.

Caribbean people usually buy whole nutmegs, and then grate them as they need fresh nutmeg for cooking. The spice is popular in dessert dishes but also adds flavor to meats, tubers, and eggs. In the Caribbean, as in other cuisines, it is considered well suited to dairy-based dishes.

Nutmeg is believed to have medicinal qualities in preventing strokes; former stroke victims place whole nutmegs in their mouths to ward off another stroke. In large quantities, nutmeg and mace can be poisonous as they contain the oil myristicin.

Salt

Salt as a seasoning is a relatively recent addition to meals in the Caribbean, historically speaking. Although the Caribs and Tainos probably cooked with salt water, they probably did not know how to extract salt from the water and use it on its own as a seasoning. Instead of salt, they used a sauce made from hot peppers and cassava juice. It is still the case today in the Caribbean that to flavor or season a dish, a cook will more often than not reach for hot pepper sauce over salt or any other seasoning. Despite this, there is now a region in the Caribbean famous for its salt production. Great Inagua, an island in the Bahamas, has been processing salt since the early seventeenth century and exporting it to Cuba and Hispaniola. Its vast quantities of very salty, shallow water combined with the frequent sun and wind, which evaporate the salt from the water, makes the terrain of Great Inagua very conducive to salt processing. While salt is not that popular in the Caribbean as a seasoning, it is often used, based on the European tradition, as a means of preserving, particularly in preserving fish by salting it.

Sugarcane

Sugarcane was brought to the Caribbean by Columbus and thrived in the Caribbean climate. Almost immediately, cultivation of sugarcane

Cutting sugarcane in St. Kitts. © Art Directors and TRIP/Helene Rogers.

proved to be a profitable endeavor. The demand for sugar in Europe and the American colonies contributed to radical changes in Caribbean society, its economy, and geography. Large sugar plantations became the dominant organization of land in many islands, and slaves were imported from Africa to work the fields. In total, about five million slaves were brought from Africa to the Caribbean, most arriving during the eighteenth century at the height of Caribbean sugar production. European plantation holders became so wealthy from profits made from sugar, and the sugar plantation system came to have such a stronghold on the Caribbean economy, that the substance of sugar came to be called liquid gold, white gold, and King sugar. By the 1850s, however, most Caribbean islands had freed their slaves, and plantation owners needed a cheap labor source to continue making profits. Indentured servants from India and China were brought to the Caribbean for terms of usually five years, but these workers would normally leave the plantations at the end of their terms. By the mid-nineteenth century, sugarcane was no longer a very profitable crop; only a few islands today still have any significant sugarcane production.

Before sugarcane is made into sugar, it must undergo a lengthy process of refinement. First the canes must be cut, ground, and squeezed in order to extract the juice. Lime juice is then added to the liquid and impurities are filtered out of it. Then, the juice has to be boiled down to a syrup and left to settle into crystals. At the end of the process, two products are left: molasses and brown sugar. Brown sugar is put through an additional refinement process to produce the white sugar that is popularly used. Molasses is still used in baked goods. Many people say that the molasses of Barbados is superior because it is unsulphured and has a very intense caramel flavor. When consumers in the Caribbean buy sugar, they ask the grocer about the color of the sugar that has been shipped to the store. The darker the color of the sugar, the less sweet it is; white sugar that has been refined outside of the Caribbean and imported back to it is typically the standard sugar used in homes.

Many Caribbean people who live in rural areas near sugarcane crops, or those who shop at farmers' markets where cane is sometimes sold fresh, enjoy sucking the sweet juice directly out of the sugarcane stalk. Most fresh sugarcane is available already peeled, but if not, it can be squeezed to yield its juice. For eating fresh sugarcane, the stalk is cut into manageable lengths and the hard skin peeled away. It is sliced into strips and chewed to remove the sweet juice. The chewed-up remains of the stalk are discarded once the juice is gone.

Thyme (Thymus Vulgaris)

This herb is in the same family as mint. It is indigenous to the Mediterranean area and was brought by European immigrants to the Caribbean. Favored in Spanish-, French-, and Portuguese-influenced Caribbean cooking, it is most frequently used in the preparation of meat dishes, but also to flavor soups, stews, and even salads. Some variations of jerk seasoning mixes include thyme.

Vanilla (Vanilla Planifolia)

The vanilla plant is in the same family as the orchid. Indigenous to the tropical rain forests of South America, vanilla now grows throughout the Caribbean. After it flowers, the vanilla plant develops green pods that contain the vanilla beans. Indigenous peoples in South America and the Caribbean not only cultivated vanilla, but they cured it to use as a flavoring in food and drinks, most notably in their drinks made from the cacao bean (otherwise known as chocolate). The curing process of the green vanilla bean involves stopping the growing process through boiling, and then drying the beans to cause fermentation. The drying process involves sun-drying the beans in the daytime, and at night wrapping the beans in blankets in order to make them sweat. Production takes anywhere from three to six months.

Vanilla pods are typically sold in glass tubes and should not look withered or dried out. The pods are best used by being cut in half lengthwise; the seeds can serve various purposes as flavoring in desserts or in sauces, and the pods can be added to an older, dark rum to produce vanilla rum. Vanilla rum works well as a substitute for vanilla extract in recipes.

COOKING OILS

Almost nothing is prepared in a Jamaican kitchen without the use of coconut oil. The peanut, native to South America and the Caribbean, also produces an oil (and a margarine made from this oil) that is used in Caribbean cooking. However, the French, Spanish, and Portuguese influence on regions in the Caribbean account for the widespread use of olive oil as well.

Palm oil is an oil derived from the juice of fruits of the oil palm tree. It is quite nutritious and is used in cooking, even in making soups and stews. Palm oil is actually a solid form of fat and can be heated in a saucepan to liquefy it for use as an oil in most recipes. Most fats used in Caribbean cooking, with the exception of olive oil, are high in saturated fat.

FRUITS AND VEGETABLES

The abundance and variety of tropical fruits in the Caribbean astounded early European explorers, and they have still remained popular export products. Most Caribbean people buy fresh fruits at markets. Still, as a special treat around Christmastime, many Caribbean households look forward to imports of fruits from around the world that do not grow in their climate.

Fresh fruits in Caribbean cuisine are baked or stewed as desserts or eaten raw as snacks. Pastes made from fruit are popular treats and are available in slabs sold wrapped in plastic or in tins. The juices of fresh fruits are typically used in drinks consumed throughout the day at almost any meal. Often, every part of a fruit tree is used, including the wood and leaves.

Fresh fruits and vegetables have always been central to the Caribbean diet. The landscape and climate create excellent conditions for a large variety of fruit and vegetable-bearing trees and plants to thrive. During slavery in the Caribbean, slaves were often fed mostly on fruits, vegetables, and legumes, and rarely given meat, because these items are very cheap and nutritious food sources. Many Caribbean people have gardens in their yards where they grow their own fruits and vegetables, and mothers often teach their children how to cultivate the homegrown produce. A typical kitchen garden in the Western Caribbean may contain cucumber, pumpkin, pigeon peas, tomatoes, sweet potatoes, yams, and any number of fruit trees.

Fruits and vegetables are often featured in traditional Caribbean art. Still life arrangements, market scenes, and landscape paintings depicting crop harvesting and cultivation are popular scenes and images in the visual art of the Caribbean, particularly in the folk art works of Haitian painters, which are popular tourist items.

Ackee (Blighia Sapida)

The scientific name of this fruit ("*Blighia*") honors Captain Bligh, who brought it from West Africa to the Caribbean at the end of the eighteenth century. It is also known as akee, vegetable brain, or achee. Ackee is one of the many foods brought to the Caribbean during the slave trade with Africa. Although it is a fruit, it is used more like a vegetable in Caribbean cooking. It is found throughout the Caribbean but has been most abundantly cultivated in Jamaica, where it is part of the national dish, ackee and salt fish. This is a kind of ackee scramble made with soaked, flaked salt cod, onions, tomatoes, scallions, and the ackee. The interior flesh of the ackee resembles scrambled eggs when cooked.

The tree on which ackee grows is an evergreen native to West Africa. The fruit is red and triangular shaped, looking a little like a pink mango or guava. It splits into three parts when it has ripened and exposes a yellow flesh with black seeds. An unripe ackee is poisonous and consumption of it could lead to "Jamaica poisoning," which often results in death. For this reason, it is featured in a popular Jamaican riddle: "My father sent me out to pick out a wife; he told me to take only those that smile, for those that do not smile will kill me. What is my wife?" Stories are told about slaves offering the fruit to their masters in its poisonous form.

In the United States, ackee can usually only be found in a can as fresh ackee is not allowed to be imported. Canned ackee can be sautéed or used as is in many recipes calling for ackee. To prepare fresh ackee for use in

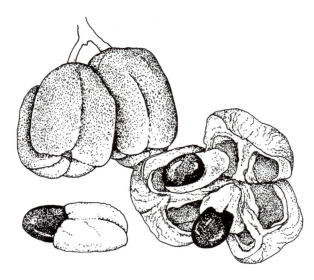

Ackee.

cooking, the shell, seed, and membrane are separated from the whitish flesh. Then, the flesh is usually soaked in water or boiled.

Avocado (Persea Americana Mill)

Avocados are called pears or alligator pears in the Caribbean, and in the Spanish Caribbean they are called *aguacate*. Although they are actually a fruit, native to South America, avocados are most frequently eaten like a vegetable in salads, as an appetizer before the main dish, or used to make a mousse. Besides being eaten, avocados are used for other purposes: the halved fruit is often used as a decorative bowl for serving seafood salads, and the leaves of the tree are made into a tea to help reduce blood pressure.

Banana (Family Musaceae)

Bananas actually grow on large herbaceous plants, not trees. They are served in the Caribbean as the first course in a large breakfast, in fruit salads, and in desserts. Bananas sprinkled with nutmeg and baked briefly in a greased casserole make a popular and easy dessert when topped with a sweet, rum-based sauce. Banana leaves are often used as wraps in which to steam, poach, or bake foods in order to impart a rich flavor. The fruit is picked from the plant when it is green, and it is then allowed to ripen. The French Caribbean word for banana is figue.

Barbados Cherry (Malpighia Glabra)

This cherry is also known as the West Indian cherry, cerise, acerola, nance, or sour cherry. The fruits are harvested from April to July. It has a very sharp taste and is rarely eaten raw, but it is used to make drinks, jams, jellies, preserves, ice cream, and puddings. The small tree on which Barbados cherries grow is a common bush in gardens and yards in the Caribbean.

Bell Peppers (Capsicum Annuum)

Bell peppers, otherwise known as sweet peppers to distinguish them from hot peppers, are greatly used in Chinese-influenced Caribbean food as well as in the sautéed dishes of Cuban cooking. The red bell pepper is actually the ripe version of the green bell pepper.

Other peppers substituted for bell peppers in Caribbean recipes are cachuca peppers (known as *ají dulce* or *rocotillo* peppers in the Spanish Caribbean); they are generally much smaller than a bell pepper but are not hot like chili peppers.

Breadfruit (Artocarpus Altilis or Artocarpus Communis)

Breadfruit, a green vegetable with lumpy skin related to the mulberry, is called *fruit à pain* in the French-speaking Caribbean. Breadfruit gets its name from its bread-like consistency when cooked. It can be baked, grilled, fried, or boiled and is often cooked like a potato or like a squash or used as substitutes for these in recipes. Breadfruit is served as a vegetable accompaniment to a main course, but it is also made into breads, pies, and

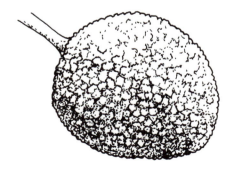

Breadfruit.

puddings. The mutiny on the *H.M.S. Bounty* was supposedly caused by breadfruit. The ship's captain, Captain Bligh, was so concerned about the safety of his breadfruit cargo that his watering of the cargo during a water shortage on the ship caused his crew to mutiny.

Breadfruit can be thrown on a fire and roasted whole; this is one of the most popular methods for preparing it in the Caribbean. After it is roasted, it is cut open and the inside flesh is taken out and served like a potato. One of the most prized varieties of breadfruits is found in Jamaica's Portland Parish and is called yellow heart breadfruit.

Breadfruit Rundown used to be made with a mixture of salted pig's tail, pig's feet, and salt beef, but today it is just made with ham. This favorite dish of Trinidad and Tobago, as well as Barbados, can be served as a meal on its own, but it is also popularly served as an accompaniment to fish dishes.

Breadfruit Rundown

- 12 oz. smoked ham, diced
- 1 tbs. vegetable oil
- 2 medium white or yellow onions, minced
- 2 garlic cloves, minced
- 1 hot chili pepper, seeds removed, minced
- 1 bunch green onions, including tops, chopped
- 2 tsp. fresh thyme, minced
- 3 c. coconut milk
- 2 small breadfruit, peeled and cut into chunks (or, alternatively, 4 chayote squash, peeled, parboiled, and cut into chunks, and 4 large baking potatoes, peeled and cut into chunks)
- salt and pepper to taste

In a large skillet over medium heat, heat the oil. Add the onion, garlic, hot pepper, green onions, and thyme. Sauté for about 5 minutes, stirring constantly. Add the coconut milk and heat briefly, then add the breadfruit (or, alternatively, the chayote and potatoes), diced ham, salt, and pepper. Reduce the heat to low and simmer, covered, until the ingredients have absorbed almost all of the coconut milk (about 40 minutes or longer). Serve hot. Makes 6–8 servings.

Callaloo (Xanthosoma Species)

Callaloo is a green, leafy vegetable and also the name of a spicy soup dish using this vegetable (this soup is known as the national dish of Trinidad and Tobago). Callaloo is also found with alternative spellings, *calalou* or *calau*. There are at least two different leafy vegetables that are referred to by the name callaloo in the Caribbean: the leaves of the plant called dasheen (elsewhere *taro* or *malanga*) and the green vegetable known as *chou Caribe* (also known as Chinese spinach, Indian kale, or *bhaji*). It seems that these names can be broken down by region: in the Eastern Caribbean, callaloo means the leaves of the taro plant, but in the Western Caribbean, callaloo means Chinese spinach or Indian kale, prepared as one would spinach or turnip/collard greens. While the leaves of the taro plant are a green leafy vegetable, the tubers of the taro, also known as tannia, or dasheen, can be treated like a potato and cut into slivers and fried.

If callaloo is not available for use in a recipe, fresh spinach may be substituted. Taro leaves need to be well cooked (at least 45 minutes). They harbor calcium oxilate residues that will cause an allergic reaction if not destroyed by cooking.

Cassava (Manihot Esculenta)

Cassava is also known as yucca, manioc, Brazilian arrowroot, or tapioca, and is the edible tuber of a plant related to the poinsettia. Native to tropical areas in the Americas, it was a staple of the Taino and Carib diet, especially in the form of cassava bread. The tuber has a thick brown skin covering white flesh and it is used to derive tapioca. The inside of the yucca is white, and it turns yellow when cooked. It is slightly sweet and chewy. It is frequently used as a potato substitute in soups and stews. It can also be fried, grilled, or steamed. Many recipes call for it to be grated. A concoction of boiled-down cassava juice combined with other spices is known as *cassareep* (a cooking sauce used since indigenous times), the key ingredient in the classic Caribbean stew called pepperpot.

Wild cassava, the bitter variety, is poisonous due to its high concentration of a prussic acid, hydrocyanic glucoside; however, the indigenous peoples of the Caribbean developed a method of extracting the poison. It is said that Taino Indians used the poisonous cassava as a method of suicide, eating the uncooked cassava to escape oppression and torture at the hands of the Spanish Conquistadors. They also used this poison to tip their spears and arrows. After peeling the tubers of the bitter cassava, they must be washed thoroughly. Before using grated cassava, it should be soaked overnight. Sweet cassava can be eaten raw without the precautions necessary for the bitter variety.

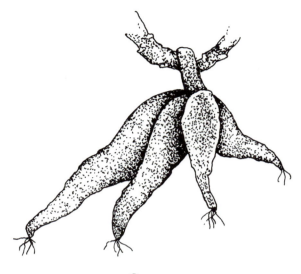

Cassava.

Cassava is a rich, complex carbohydrate and is used as a base from which to make beer. In traditional preparation, after cassava has been grated and boiled to remove toxins, the meat is chewed to convert it from starch to sugar by contact with saliva and its enzymes. Then, it is spit out into a pot, mixed with water, and left to ferment.

Cassava bread is eaten throughout the Caribbean. In the French islands, it is called *pain de kassav*. In the Spanish islands, it is known as *pan de casabe*.

Chayote (Sechium Edule)

The chayote is also known as a vegetable pear, *choyotae*, cho-cho, choko, and squash. In Jamaica, it is called a chocho; in Louisiana, a *mirliton;* and in France and the Francophone Caribbean, it is known as *christophene*. Chayotes originated in Mexico and were brought to the Caribbean in the eighteenth century. A member of the gourd family, the chayote is the size and shape of a large, flattened pear, and ranges in color from white to light green. It tastes like a combination of squash and eggplant and is used much like zucchini: grated raw in salads, stuffed and baked, sautéed, steamed, or stir-fried. In Jamaica, as the texture is similar to that of an apple, the chayote is even used to make a filling for pies. The large central seed of the young chayote is also edible and can be cooked with the rest of the chayote.

Chayotes are available in specialty grocery stores, especially in the wintertime. Firm, unblemished small fruits are the most tender. They can be stored up to a month in the refrigerator. For large chayotes, the skin can be peeled with a potato peeler before cooking, or by just pulling the skin off after the chayote is cooked. Chayotes will develop a mushy texture if overcooked.

Coconut (Cocos Nucifera)

Despite what its name suggests, the coconut is not a nut, but the fruit of the coco palm tree. The shell of the coconut is waterproof, and this fact has permitted the fruits to travel by water to reproduce themselves in many tropical areas, including the Caribbean.

In Caribbean food preparation, all parts of the coconut are utilized (and the leaves of the coconut palm are useful for thatching roofs). The shells serve as containers, the sap goes into drinks, and coconut meat and milk are used in making a variety of famous Caribbean dishes, like coconut fudge (made with coconut milk, sugar, butter, rum, and vanilla extract), which is served throughout the Caribbean, Barbados's coconut custard pie, Puerto Rico's *tembleque*, and Jamaica's coconut tart. Coconut chips are popular salty accompaniments to alcoholic beverages, especially those made with rum. To make these chips, coconut meat is thinly sliced, baked on baking sheets, and then sprinkled with salt while still hot.

Sweet Coconut Bread

- 2 c. grated coconut flakes (sweetened)
- 1 c. sugar
- 2 eggs, beaten
- 1 c. evaporated milk
- 1 tsp. pure vanilla extract
- 1/2 tsp. ground cinnamon
- 1/4 c. seedless raisins
- 1/2 c. rum or water
- 2 tbs. salted, sweet cream butter, melted

- 3 c. flour
- 1 tbs. baking powder

Heat rum or water in saucepan for a few minutes, but do not boil. Place raisins in a metal or glass bowl and pour rum or water over them. Soak raisins for 10 minutes.

In large bowl, combine coconut and sugar. Drain raisins and reserve rum, if used, for use in another recipe. In another bowl, combine eggs, evaporated milk, vanilla, cinnamon, drained raisins, and butter. Stir this mixture into the grated coconut and egg mixture. Sift in flour, baking powder, and salt. Mix until batter is smooth. Pour batter into two greased 8-inch loaf pans, bake at 350° for 1 hour, or until tester comes out clean. Set pans on wire rack to cool for 10 minutes. Remove the breads from pans and continue cooling on wire racks. Makes 2 loaves—do not halve recipe. Serve with jelly as a snack.

Djon Djon Mushrooms (Psathyrella Genus)

The word "djon djon" in Haitian Creole means simply fungus. These small shitake-flavored mushrooms are a specialty of Northern Haiti. Rice dishes are made from these mushrooms and from water in which they have been cooked. One of these dishes, *riz djon djon*, is traditionally served with the Haitian pork dish *griots*, accompanied by *banane pesé*, fried plantain, and the Haitian hot pepper sauce *ti-malice*. The other dish, *riz noir*, is traditionally served at special occasions like birthdays, weddings, and religious ceremonies.

Eggplant (Solanum Melongena)

The eggplant was introduced to the Caribbean by East Indians and is related to the potato. It is also called aubergine, egg fruit, garden egg, mad apple, *melongene*, and *brinjal*. In Trinidad, it is used to make the famous *baigani*, a type of fritter. Lebanese immigrants to regions of the Caribbean use the eggplant in their dip *baba ganoush*. In other Caribbean recipes, it is usually boiled, fried, or grilled; it is also often stuffed with meat mixtures and baked.

Eggplant Fritters

- 2 c. eggplant, peeled and cubed
- 2 tsp. lemon juice
- 3/4 c. lightly salted water

- 1 egg, beaten
- 2 scallions, finely chopped
- 2 tsp. chopped fresh parsley
- 1 1/2 tsp. garlic powder
- 1 1/2 tsp. chili powder
- 1 1/2 tsp. salt
- 1 tsp. black pepper
- dash white pepper
- 1/2 tsp. cumin
- 5 tbs. flour
- 1/2 tsp. baking powder
- salt and pepper
- vegetable oil

Place eggplant, lemon juice, and salted water in a saucepan and heat over medium heat until eggplant is tender (about 10 or 15 minutes). Strain eggplant in a colander and puree in a food processor. In a separate bowl, beat egg, and then add scallion, parsley, garlic powder, chili powder, salt, black and white pepper, and cumin. Stir, then add flour, baking powder, and eggplant puree. Heat enough oil in a heavy pot to cover about 1 inch of the bottom. Scoop batter up with a tablespoon and drop it in the oil. Make sure batter does not burn to the bottom of the pot. Deep fry until golden brown on both sides. Drain on paper towels and salt to taste. Serve hot. Makes about 20 fritters.

Guava (Psidium Guajava)

Native to South America and the Caribbean, the trees on which guavas grow as fruit are related to the clove and bay trees. The word guava is from the Taino language, but it is also known by the name guayaba, and, in Haiti, *guayaru*. Guavas tend to vary in size, shape, color, and taste depending on the individual variety of the fruit throughout the Caribbean. The months of October, November, and December are harvest time for guavas. Both ripe and unripe guavas are eaten in the Caribbean. Unripe guavas are tart and may be used for jams, jellies, chutneys, and other condiments. Ripe guavas are sweet and can be used in a number of dessert recipes (possibly baked or stewed) or just enjoyed raw. They are often consumed for breakfast as a first course. Because guavas contain many small, hard seeds in their flesh, most people just make them into jams and jellies or use them for their juice. In the Spanish Caribbean, the shell of the guava (the outer coating) is poached in sugar syrup and served as dessert with a soft cheese. A medicinal tea used to cure diarrhea is made from the leaves and bark of the guava tree.

Guinep (Mellicoccus Bijungatus)

Guinep are harvested during the summer months and are eaten like grapes. Their flesh is translucent orange-yellow and of the consistency of jelly. For recipes, the tough, thin skin is sliced off and the inside flesh and seeds are put into a pot of boiling water for 15–20 minutes. Both the water and the boiled fruit are used for making jelly. The seeds can also be eaten by baking or roasting them.

Hearts of Palm

Hearts of palm are the hearts of the palm tree. In the Caribbean, they are eaten fresh; the husks are removed, and they are boiled in water with a

Guinep.

little lemon juice, drained, and served as a salad with vinaigrette dressing, in fritters, or accompanying asparagus topped with hollandaise sauce.

Jackfruit (Artocarpus Heterophyllus)

Jackfruit is related to the breadfruit and is in the same family as the fig. The fruit looks very similar to breadfruit, as both have a green color and an oval shape, and both have bumpy skin. The way to tell the difference between them is that jackfruit grows very close to the bark of the tree. The fruits are large and heavy and are sold in parts or cut up into pieces. They can be eaten fresh or put into salads. Jackfruit is made into a curry in the Indian immigrant community and served at weddings and special occasions. The seeds inside the flesh can be roasted whole and eaten as nuts. The flesh of the jackfruit is consumed both raw and cooked, similar in preparation to the breadfruit, although the latter is a more popular food choice.

Lime (Citrus Aurantifolia)

Limes come from the Indo-Malaysian region but are now found growing in most tropical areas and warmer climates. European explorers brought lime trees to the Caribbean, and they have become an integral component of Caribbean cuisine in sauces, in vegetable dishes, in almost every manner of fish and shellfish preparation, in the preparation of poultry, and even in the preparation of beef (in Cuban cooking), as well as desserts and alcoholic mixed drinks. Limes are ripe when they are light yellow; when they are past their prime they turn bright yellow. Because limes go bad very quickly, they are picked when they are still green. British sailors discovered that limes were an excellent cure for the sickness they experienced on long sea voyages, known eventually as scurvy. Limes are an important ingredient in Jamaican cooking, especially sauces and marinades.

Mammee Apple (Mammea Americana)

This fruit is also known as mamey or St. Domingo apricot, and it is indigenous to the Caribbean. It is the fruit of an evergreen tree and was eaten regularly by Amerindians. The meat of the mammee apple looks like that of apricot except that it has a few large seeds in it. It has a sweet reddish-orange flesh and is popularly used as an ingredient to make milkshakes and ice cream. The mammee is used in many forms of drinks—those made from fruit juices, and also alcoholic mixed drinks. Like most fruits, it is eaten raw as a snack, or it is stewed or baked and used to create desserts. Also like other fruits, it is made into jams and jellies, and preserves are made from greener versions of the fruits.

Mango (Mangifera Indica)

The mango is referred to in the Caribbean as the king of the fruits and the peach of the tropics. Related to the pistachio and cashew, the tree arrived in Brazil in the fifteenth century from India, and in the Caribbean sometime near the end of the nineteenth century.

Both green and ripe mangoes are used in Caribbean cuisine. Green mango can be used in the preparation of desserts, as its flesh is similar to that of an apple and can be used as filling for pies. Unripe mangos may also serve as accompaniments to sauces, like the chutneys of the British-Indian Caribbean, and can even be prepared in a curry. In the French Caribbean, *rougail de mangue verte* is a spicy relish made from unripe mangos, while in Trinidad and Tobago, pickled green mangos are a popular snack. Relishes and chutneys made from both ripe and unripe mangos frequently accompany salty meats. Ripe mangoes are most frequently served fresh for breakfast or in fruit salads and are also used in a variety of desserts such as mango pie, mango brown Betty, and mango mousse.

Mangos are ripe when they are soft to the touch, fragrant, and when their outer skin turns pink or yellow and has light brown flecks. The inside meat is a yellow-orange color and a little fibrous. Some varieties of mangos stay greenish even when ripe.

Naseberry (Manilkara Zapota)

This fruit is otherwise known as the sapodilla, marmale plum, beef apple, and nispero, and is indigenous to South America and the Caribbean. The sap from the tree of this fruit is extracted and used in the production of chewing gum. The flesh of the naseberry is translucent and has many small dark seeds. The small round fruit has reddish-brown skin.

Okra (Hibiscus Esculentus)

Okra, another food item brought to the Caribbean from Africa during the slave trade, is known by many names in the Caribbean: gumbo, *gombo* (in French speaking countries), *giamba* (on Dutch islands), okro, ochro, achro, *quingombo* (in Puerto Rico), *malondron* (in the Dominican Republic), *bindi* (in Trinidad and Jamaica), *bamie,* and lady's fingers. Used to thicken sauces and soups, it has become a key ingredient in many popular and traditional dishes in the Caribbean, such as callaloo and pepperpot. Combined with cornmeal, it is also eaten in a cornmeal dish called coo-coo, or cou-cou (which can also mean simply side dish). It may be used in salads or just served as a vegetable to accompany main dishes. The plant is related to the hibiscus. The fruit comes from pods that are ripe only three months after being planted. Okra seeds can be roasted and used in place of coffee. The leaves of the okra plant, the fruit pods, and the unripened fruits are used medicinally, as okra is believed to treat various ailments from eye problems to reproductive problems.

Ortanique (Rutaceae Family)

Jamaica and a few other islands in the Caribbean produce this citrus fruit in large quantities for commercial export. Ortanique is a naturally occurring hybrid between the tangerine and the orange. Its juice and zest are used in baking and for preserves. The juice is used to make a glaze for Caribbean rum cake (also known as black cake).

Papaya (Carica Papaya)

Papaya, indigenous to the Caribbean, is also called papaw or pawpaw. It is known as *fruta bomba* in Cuba, *lechosa* in the Dominican Republic and Puerto Rico, and *papaye* in the French-speaking Caribbean. When Columbus noted in his journal that the natives ate frequently of a tree that produced "fruit of angels," he was referring to the papaya. Papaya slices are eaten for breakfast in the Caribbean with lime juice on them. Papaya is also used in sauces, as condiments, or fresh in salads. It is often used to tenderize meat and contains the enzyme papain, which aids in digestion; for instance, meat can be tenderized by being wrapped in leaves of the papaya tree, as these too contain papain. The leaves of the papaya can also be used as a green, leafy vegetable. In Africa, green papaya was substituted in recipes when eggplant was not available, so Africans in the Caribbean began the tradition of using green papaya in the place of a vegetable in Caribbean dishes.

Passion Fruit (Passiflora Edulis)

This Caribbean fruit was named by early Spanish Conquistadors in the Americas. The name they gave it, passion fruit, had religious connotations and was chosen because various parts of the plant and fruit seemed to symbolize important figures and elements involved with Christ's crucifixion. Spanish explorers, in particular, were eager to find signs that God was behind their mission to colonize the New World and convert its inhabitants to Christianity.

Passion fruit is the fruit from the passionflower and looks a little like a plum. The plant on which the fruit grows is a vine-like species. The fruit is oval shaped and has a purplish brown skin when ripe has the consistency of thin leather. The flesh of the berry is found in small sacks surrounded by edible seeds. It is gelatinous, golden-colored, and has a very floral bouquet and a sweet, citrus taste. Its tart flesh is yellow or orange in color and is used in sorbets and other desserts. The fruit is most often consumed in its fresh state by cutting it in half and spooning out and eating the inside flesh with a spoon. Passion fruit juice is commonly used in both alcoholic and non-alcoholic drinks. Also known as *ceibey* in some areas, in the French-speaking Caribbean it is called *maracudja* or *granadille*, and in the Spanish-speaking Caribbean it is called *granadilla*.

Pineapple (Ananas Comosus)

Pineapples are indigenous to South America and the Caribbean. Columbus found them being cultivated in Haiti. The Caribs called them *anana*, meaning fragrance or fragrant fruit. Because the pineapples looked like pinecones to the early Spanish explorers, they named them *piña de los Indias* (Indian pinecone) or *piña* for short. The English later added the word "apple" to its name because this at the time was a general term for any fruit. Pineapples contain no starch and therefore do not ripen after they are picked. They must be taken off the tree in the peak of their ripeness for the best flavor. Pineapples can be served with or used in the preparation of meats since the fruit aids in the digestion of proteins. In many dessert recipes, the fruit is often paired with coconut.

Plantain (Musa Paradisiaca)

Plantains are also referred to as green bananas, but they are different from bananas in that they have a higher starch content and are less sweet. Plantains can be consumed in their unripe state (when they are green), but they must be cooked. However, different dishes require plantains in different stages of ripeness. Plantains are served in many ways throughout the Caribbean, sometimes as a sweet food and sometimes salty. They can be grilled, fried, boiled, broiled, pressed, pureed, baked, or barbecued. Fried plantain frequently accompanies meat dishes in the Caribbean; for instance, double fried plantain, known as *tostones* in the Spanish speaking Caribbean, joins with chopped beef and cheese to make the Puerto Rican dish *piononos*, and in Haiti, where fried plantains are known as *bananes pesées*, they are traditionally served with griyo (see Chapter 6 for recipe).

Twice-fried Plantains

- Plantains, peeled, and cut into round slices of about 1/2 thick (2 plantains serve about 4 people)
- Salt
- Water
- Vegetable oil

Place plantain slices in a large bowl and cover them with salted water. Let sit for 30 minutes. Drain (reserving salted water) and remove any moisture from the slices by patting with paper towels. Heat one inch of oil in a large frying pan (the oil is hot enough when a plantain slice makes a sizzling sound when it comes in contact with the oil) and add only as many plantain slices as can fit in a single layer in the pan. Fry slices on both sides until tender and only slightly browned (about 2 minutes each side). Remove from pan with slotted spoon and drain on paper towels. Lay plantain slices between two pieces of waxed paper and flatten them down with your palm or with the bottom of a soup can until they are half their original thickness. Dip the plantain slices in the salted water again, pat dry, and reheat the oil. Fry the slices in the pan again on both sides until golden brown and crispy (about 3-4 minutes each side). Drain on paper towels and salt to taste. Serve hot.

Pomegranate (Punica Granatum)

The pomegranate, also known as the apple of Carthage, is round, about the size of an orange, and its thick, leathery skin is yellowish-red in color when ripe. Inside the skin are many small white seeds surrounded by translucent flesh. Its juice is used in making the drink grenadine.

Pumpkin (Cucurbita Maxima)

Pumpkins cooked in the Caribbean are not the same kind that are used throughout North America for pies and carving in the fall, although they are also in the gourd family. The outside of Caribbean pumpkins (known as winter squash, *calabaza, calebasse, giromon* or *giraumon*) are usually greenish or yellow in color (dark yellow when ripe), and specked with white. They may be round or oval in shape. Their bright yellow flesh is used to make soups or to serve mashed or stuffed. Because they are rather large, they are most often sold in pieces, not whole.

Seagrape (Coccoloba Uvifera)

The fruit may have been one of the first plants viewed by Columbus. Seagrapes are sour but have high amounts of pectin, so they are often made into jellies and jams. Also, they can be made into a cold soup.

Sorrel (Hibiscus Sabdariffa)

This annual plant is also called *roselle*, Jamaican sorrel, Indian sorrel, or red sorrell and is related to the hibiscus. Its sepals are used as fruits. Because it blooms in late November and early December, sorrel is used in many aspects of Christmas festivities in the Caribbean. The sorrel fruits are soaked in water with other flavorings as a drink, or fermented and added to rum. The seeds are used in jams and jellies.

Sour Orange (Citrus Aurantium)

This Asian citrus fruit brought to the Caribbean by European immigrants (perhaps with many of the other citrus fruits introduced to the Caribbean by Columbus) is also known as bitter orange, Seville orange, or, in Spanish, as *naranja agria*. The sour orange is smaller than a regular orange and its juice is used in Spanish Caribbean sauces and marinades, especially for meat dishes, and in the Cuban seasoning *adobo*. It was initially brought to the Dutch Caribbean in an attempt to develop agriculture on the island of Curacao. Nothing could be grown in the poor soil there, and the oranges were abandoned and left to grow wild. Later, it was discovered that the descendants of these Seville oranges, called *Lahara* locally, contained a fragrant, etheric oil in their peels, and the orange-flavored Curacao liquor was born.

Soursop (Annona Muricata)

Soursop, known as *corossol* in French, *guanabana* in Spanish, and also prickly custard apple in English, was brought from South America to the

Caribbean in the sixteenth century. It looks somewhat like an artichoke, with a green, prickly skin, and the flesh of its fruit is a light pink or white with a sweet, acidic flavor and a custard-like consistency. The fruit is consumed raw, or used raw in juices, sorbets, ice creams, custards, and candies. The flesh turns to a creamy pulp when added to a liquid like water or milk, which makes it a very popular fruit base for drinks, including alcoholic mixed drinks. The seeds of the soursop are toxic and cannot be eaten. To use fresh soursop in desserts, the fruit should be peeled, the membrane taken out, and the seed discarded.

Shaddock (Citrus Grandis)

Although it tends to be larger, less bitter, and shaped more like a pear, the shaddock is a citrus fruit related to the grapefruit. It is also known as a pummelo and in French it is called *chadec*. This fruit was brought from Southeast Asia to Barbados in the seventeenth century, supposedly by a Captain Shaddock from whom it received its name. Usually it is eaten fresh, the pulp is used for juice, and its rind is candied like that of other citrus fruits.

Starfruit (Averrhoa Carambola)

Also named carambola, this native Asian fruit is shaped with five outer ridges. When sliced along its width, a piece of starfruit looks like a star,

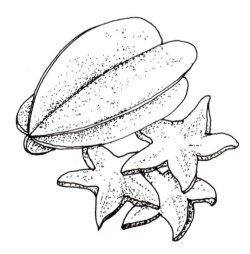

Starfruit.

with five points. It may be used in the Caribbean in salads or eaten raw, but it is most often used as a garnish on plates, glasses, and serving trays.

Sweet Potato (Ipomoea Batatas)

When Columbus tasted the sweet potato during his first voyage to the Caribbean—in salads, cooked with pork, and soaked in almond milk—he thought he was eating yams. He called them *ñames*, in Spanish, from the West African name for yams (*nyami*). Sweet potatoes are often confused with yams but are in fact from a different plant species. They grow on a perennial plant and have a pink skin and off-white flesh. They can be baked or mashed and have a roasted, nutty taste. A yam is a thicker, heavier tuber with flesh that varies from white to purple.

In the Caribbean today, sweet potatoes are consumed in a variety of forms such as breads, soups, candies, pastries, and pies. In the French Caribbean, they are called *patates douces* and in the Spanish Caribbean, *patatas dulces*. Cooks in the Spanish Caribbean make a sweetened paste from the sweet potato, often flavored with chocolate or vanilla, and eat it as a snack or dessert.

Tamarind (Tamarindus Indica)

The tamarind is the fruit from the pod of an evergreen tree indigenous to India. The Tamarind tree grows a brown pod from which a pulp is extracted and then processed to be used as flavoring. Originally, these trees were planted in the Caribbean as barriers against wind. Now, the unripe fruits are used as seasoning in curries and its ripe fruits are often made into a candy that has a sweet yet spicy taste. It is most famous as an ingredient in Angostura Bitters, a mixer for alcoholic drinks, but is also used in other varieties of refreshing drinks. In its naturally tart state, without the addition of sugar, it is used as a seasoning for fish or meat dishes. In fact,

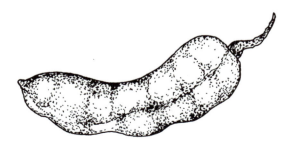

Tamarind.

the tamarind is one of the main ingredients in Worcestershire sauce, a British sauce used on cooked meats and also as a marinade. Tangy sweet ball-shaped candies made from the pulp can be found throughout markets in the Caribbean as a favorite dessert; the taste of these tamarind balls provides a unique marriage of Caribbean flavors, adding garlic and hot pepper to an otherwise sweet snack.

Tomato (Lycopersicon Esculentum)

Although the tomato is generally used in Caribbean cooking like a vegetable, it is really a fruit. In the Dominican Republic, however, it is used like a fruit in a popular pudding-type dessert called *dulce de tomate* (candied tomato). Cinnamon, normally considered a "sweet" spice used in desserts, may frequently be added as a flavor to tomato-based dishes in Caribbean cooking.

Ugli Fruit (Citrus Family)

This hybrid citrus fruit is also called hoogly in its native Jamaica. It is a cross between the tangerine, the Seville orange, the grapefruit, and perhaps the mandarin orange. Its size is that of a large grapefruit, and it has very wrinkled, easy-to-peel skin that ranges from greenish to light orange in color.

Yam (Dioscorea Family)

Yams are also called by various names sounding like the African word *nyami*, meaning "something to eat"; in French, the yam is called *igname*, and in Spanish, it is called *ñame*. Yams are treated like potatoes in cuisine and often confused with sweet potatoes. Different regions of the Caribbean have different names for yams, and often local varieties of yams are referred to by individual names; for instance, in Trinidad and Tobago, yams are called cushcush, and a preferred tropical yam in the Caribbean is called boniato. Not as sweet as an American sweet potato, but still as rich in beta-carotene, the boniato has a red skin and dry, white flesh.

GRAINS AND FLOURS

In the Caribbean, foods made from grains, such as breads, used to be considered staples of the lower classes' diet. Nowadays, however, grain foods are widely accepted across classes as part of Caribbean food culture, as they are a major component of the diets of many of the immigrant groups to the Caribbean. Snacks that are contained by bread, or that are eaten using bread as a utensil, are popular with street vendors throughout the Caribbean and reflect regional differences. However, this should not suggest that breads and other grain foods are not made at home. Any Caribbean housewife has a kitchen fully equipped for cooking homemade Caribbean grain foods, like breads (both salty and sweet), rice, and cornmeal side dishes. Many traditional Caribbean breads, however, are not made from grain flour; instead they are made from flour derived from ground legumes or tubers.

Corn

Corn, known as maize, is indigenous to the Caribbean and the Americas, but many of the dishes in the Caribbean made from cornmeal have been influenced by African styles of food preparation. Funghi (or funchi), a popular dish throughout the Caribbean, enjoyed particularly in Antigua, is either a cornmeal pudding or cake that accompanies boiled fish dishes and other main courses. A variation of this food is made in Curacao, where they eat a corn pancake, called funchi, with fillings. In Aruba, too, there is a pancake made from cornmeal and flour called pan bati. Cornmeal pudding is a favorite side dish: in Haiti it is called tum tum and in English-speaking islands it is called coo-coo (or cou-cou) and usually covered with sauce to accompany steamed fish or meat dishes. The traditional utensil used to stir this dish is called a funchi stick (see Chapter 3).

Funchi

- 1 1/2 c. cold water
- 1 c. yellow cornmeal
- 1 tsp. salt
- 1/2 c. boiling water
- 1 tbs. salted sweet cream butter

Mix cold water, cornmeal, and salt in a heavy nonstick saucepan. Stir in the boiling water and butter. Bring to a boil and cook for about 6 minutes. Stir continuously with a wooden spoon (or funchi stick). The mixture is done when it pulls away from the sides of the pan and has a stiff consistency. Remove from heat and serve immediately.

Rice

Rice was brought to the Caribbean by early Spanish explorers, but it was not seriously cultivated until the arrival of immigrants from India and China. After it is picked, it needs to be sifted in order to do away with the husks around the grains. It is used widely in dishes with peas or beans and also with Indian curries and many Chinese dishes. In Trinidad and Tobago, rice dishes are usually simple, sometimes spicy variations of steamed or boiled rice. Although rice did not become a flourishing crop in the Caribbean until about the seventeenth and eighteenth centuries, many of what are considered staple Caribbean dishes rely on rice; for example, the staple dish of rice and beans. Rice has become the essential starch of Caribbean cuisine. It is calcium-rich and supplies high amounts of iron, protein, and B vitamins.

The preferred rice in Caribbean cooking is southern Asian basmati, a type of white Asian long-grain rice. In general, Caribbean cooks use this rice or a rice of the same texture, including Indian-influenced Trinidadian cuisine. However, the Spanish influence means that some rice dishes in the Spanish Caribbean use a medium- to short-grain white rice that has a mushier texture, similar to the Italian arborio rice used to make risotto.

Breads

The East Indian influence on the Caribbean, primarily in Trinidad and Tobago, has made various kinds of breads popular. There are breads cooked on griddles, like *roti* (the actual Hindu word for bread), *paratha, chapatti, dosti,* and *sada,* all of which are made by combining flour, salt, water, and baking powder (an ingredient not normally found in breads made in India). The dough for these breads is usually quite thin and they are cooked on a flat griddle called a *tawa,* although Caribbean consumers now buy it most often frozen from grocery stores. Fried breads like floats, bakes, or *bara* are also popular in Trinidad and Tobago. Floats are traditionally served with accras; these are salt fish fritters that go by a variety of names in the Caribbean (known in Jamaica as stamp-and-go). Bakes are the bread that accompanies shark in the famous shark-and-bake of Trinidad. Bara is the bread that makes the snack called doubles, served with a chickpea filling. Baked breads are not as popular in the Indian-influenced areas of the Caribbean. However, many baked breads made with fruits or vegetables, like coconut or cassava, serve as desserts in many regions of the Caribbean.

Breads made from ground vegetables and legumes are popular in Indian-influenced Caribbean cooking. Split peas are ground to make a flour called *dahl* that is used in many baked goods. A flour is also made from green plantains that have been dried and ground. This flour is used in the preparation of fufu, a sticky dough that is fried in balls and served as a type of dumpling. Whole cornmeal is ground to make a flour; cornmeal or corn flour are also used in many baked goods, as well as porridges, and in the preparation of the dishes fungi and coo-coo, cornmeal dishes similar to the Italian polenta, or even the grits of the southern United States.

Regular cassava bread is an unleavened bread that serves as a type of cracker at meals, like a lavosh bread. It is sold in the Caribbean in plastic bags or in larger sheets wrapped in paper and tied with strings. A thicker bread made from cassava flour is called bammy or bammie. This bread is popularly eaten with fried fish and with ackee and salt fish. Because many homes in the Caribbean do not traditionally have indoor ovens, many recipes for breads are adapted for cooking on stove tops. However, one type of Caribbean bread that is baked in an oven is coco bread. These are rolls baked in an oven with a pan of water placed in the bottom of the oven in order to keep the dough moist. Another oven-baked bread is the standard Jamaican white bread known as hard-dough bread, also called hardo bread. This bread is rather dense in consistency and tends to be slightly sweet, as the top is brushed with sugar water before it is baked.

Baked Goods

Class distinctions affecting cooking methods and recipe selection can be noted in baked goods in the Caribbean. Middle- and upper-class women usually choose ingredients, recipes, and cooking techniques when they make desserts, especially sweetened baked goods, that result in lighter baked goods. The baked goods made in the households of lower-income families, however, typically tend to be heavier and sweeter and are referred to as heavy sweets.

Traditional bakery desserts include the traditional Caribbean Christmas cake known as black cake or rum cake. It is similar to fruitcake, but it has a much lighter texture. Formerly, the first step in the preparation of the dough, after soaking the dried fruits in rum, was caramelizing sugar by boiling it in water, a process probably developed by African slaves on sugar plantations. However, that step is now often left out of the recipe and the cake is made either without caramelized sugar, or with a bottled burnt-sugar flavoring, but the flavor is not as rich. Normally, steps in the process of making the cake are begun in September or October, when pieces of dried fruit are placed in rum and left to sit for about three months. However, most cooks today let the fruit sit for shorter time periods of one to two weeks, and some even shorten the time by cooking the dried fruits in the rum for about 30 minutes. Typically, then, a few days before Christmas the dough is made, the rum-soaked fruits are added, and the cake is baked.

Caribbean islanders enjoy the consumption of sweets, but their sweet tooth is influenced by European tastes, not African ones. African cuisine does not normally call for heavy sweets at the end of a meal; instead the focus is the main meal, but something simple like a piece of fruit might be consumed afterwards. Caribbean islanders not only like sweets, but they like heavy baked goods for dessert, and sometimes even for breakfast. For instance, some cake-like breads, such as coconut bread, are enjoyed for breakfast, eaten with butter or jelly.

Other types of sweet baked goods enjoyed regularly in the Caribbean are bullas, which are a type of dense, flat gingerbread cookie. Another type of cookie is known as a toto. These cookies are made slightly larger than a bulla; they are also lighter and not as crisp or as heavy. Totoes are cooked in long baking sheets and cut into squares. Besides these sweet bakery goods, there are fruit buns made with candied fruit and raisins similar to the Italian *panetone*, various kinds of tartlets, and a baked pudding called pone, which is usually made from cornmeal or yucca flour (cassava flour). The Caribbean even has its own version of scones; they are called rock cakes and made with currants and candied fruit peels and sometimes even grated coconut.

Coconut is a favorite ingredient in baked goods in the Caribbean. There are a number of macaroon-style cookies due to the amount of fresh coconut available. One popular variety is the coconut drop, which is made with both fresh coconut and fresh ginger and is cooked until the sugar develops a slightly burnt flavor. After these cookies cool, they develop a consistency almost like a candy. Red and white grater cakes are more like standard macaroons. To make grater cakes, a coconut batter is baked and then one half of it is left white and the other half is dyed red. A portion of the red mixture and a portion of the white mixture are joined and the treat is boiled like a candy.

BEANS AND LEGUMES

The Caribbean offers many varieties of beans, and its cooking relies heavily on them. Beans are highly nutritious and can be combined well with other foods to provide highly nutritious meals (for instance, when they are served with rice, baked with meats, or included in stews and soups). In the Caribbean, beans and rice are traditionally cooked together in the same pot, but since beans require a longer cooking time than rice they are put in the pot first. Beans are a very good source of vegetable protein, vitamins, and minerals, and are low in fat. In their fresh or canned form, legumes are known as beans or peas. In Jamaica, beans are also called peas. However, when they are dried, they are technically known as pulses. Beans are also available frozen in Caribbean supermarkets.

Black Beans

Black beans are a staple in the Spanish Caribbean diet, especially in Cuba, and are used often in soups and stews; for instance, in Cuba's famous black bean soup. They have less starch in them than many other beans. Like other beans, black beans are high in protein, iron, calcium, and phosphorous. Spanish Caribbean cuisine uses black beans to make sauces for dishes like those featuring seafood.

Black-Eyed Peas

Black-eyed peas are also called cow peas, and they are one of the many foods brought to the New World from Africa. Their name refers to the dark spot located on the outside flesh of the uncooked bean. They are enjoyed in a variety of bean dishes in the Caribbean, either dried or canned, and they are also ground after cooking and made into a flour. The flour is then fried to make a kind of fritter served with hot sauce. Black-eyed peas are made into fritters, which in the Dutch Caribbean are called *kalas*, and in other Caribbean islands are called calas, accras, or acara. The Caribbean names appear to be adaptations of the West African name of these fritters: *accara*. To make the black-eyed pea fritter, the peas are soaked, then ground into a dough, and fried in small balls.

Bora Beans

Also known as the bodi bean, bunchi, boonchi, Chinese bean, or snake bean, these long, rope-like beans resemble very thin, crunchy green beans and are used by all immigrant groups in dishes including curries, fried rices, chow meins, and salads. The beans grow to be very long, sometimes up to four feet in length, and have been nicknamed yard-long beans because of their length. They are most famous in a lamb dish of Aruba where they are grilled along with pieces of lamb kebab. To eat the lamb kebabs, the bora beans are removed and dipped in a spicy peanut sauce.

Chickpeas

Chickpeas, also known as garbanzos, were brought to the Americas by early Spanish and Portuguese explorers. These beans are most widely used in the cooking of Indian immigrants, who rely on chickpeas to make ground mixtures that are popular served on fried breads, like humus and *channa* (a mixture of ground chickpeas served with doubles, fried bread). Chickpeas are also frequently used in curry and are very popular in Trinidad and Tobago, the Caribbean islands with the largest concentration of immigrants from the East Indies.

Lentils

Lentils are native to South America. In Puerto Rico, they are used popularly in a tomato-based stew in which they are combined with chorizo, garlic, chili peppers, bay leaves, and coriander. Chickpeas and lentils are frequently added to salads. In Cuba, there is a favorite soup made of vegetables, rice, and lentils, flavored with white wine and spices.

Pigeon Peas

Pigeon peas are tropical green peas and a staple in Caribbean cooking; they are favored throughout the Caribbean, but especially in Cuba and Puerto Rico. Like many beans, they are paired with rice in Caribbean cooking. When paired with rice, pigeon peas are frequently cooked in coconut milk and seasoned with chili peppers. Rice and peas made with pigeon peas in the Spanish Caribbean are called *arroz con gandule*. Pigeon peas are the preferred bean to include in recipes for pepperpot and are known by many different names: gandules, goongoo, gungu pea, and cajan pea. The ripe pods of the pigeon pea normally vary from a light green to a dark brown color. The seeds can vary anywhere from gray to yellow in color. They contain high amounts of potassium, protein, fiber, and iron.

Red Beans, or Kidney Beans

The variety of kidney bean popular in the Caribbean is the small red bean, which resembles the standard kidney bean except that it has a round shape (instead of oval) and is smaller. These are the preferred beans for the Jamaican bean and rice dish called peas and rice. The name red bean is a literal translation of the French term for kidney beans: *pois rouges*.

NUTS

Many foods referred to as nuts may not technically be nuts, but would instead be classified as legumes. This is true for the almond, cashew, and peanut. However, since they are treated like edible nuts in Caribbean cooking and not like other legumes, they are classified here according to their usage and consumption as nuts. There are many other nuts and nut-like legumes consumed in the Caribbean, but these are probably the three most popular for use in food preparation and cooking.

Almonds (Terminalia Catappa)

Almonds are indigenous to African, Asian, and Mediterranean areas, and are in the same family as plums. A variety of almond, known as the bitter almond or the tropical almond, grows in the Caribbean. Almonds are used in desserts on islands like the Bahamas, where they are the base for a sweet dessert called almond cake. They are also eaten pickled (preserved in vinegar).

Cashew (Anacardium Occidentale)

Also known as caju, cajugaja, or maranon, cashews are indigenous to South America and the Caribbean but grow in many parts of the world and are now more widely cultivated in India than anywhere else. The cashew tree, from the same scientific family as the mango and poison ivy, produces a fruit known as the cashew apple, which is used in cooking like a bell pepper, made into a jelly, or even made into a fermented drink. The nut grows on the base of the apple, and it needs to be extracted from a casing in order to access the nut kernel, which is then roasted. Cashews are more expensive than many varieties of nuts because they are harvested manually. There is an oil in the nut casing that is poisonous, and when removing the nut kernel from its casing some people risk developing skin irritations or worse from contact with the poisonous oil.

Peanut (Arachis Hypogaea)

The peanut is known by the names monkeynut, earth nut, and goober-pea, but in the Caribbean its most popular name is the ground nut. Peanuts are native to the Americas and were taken to Africa by European voyagers. Slaves reintroduced peanuts to the region and the name ground nut comes from the Bantu word *nguba,* which the colonists mispronounced as goober.

The peanut plant produces small flowers above ground and then buries the seed pods underground to ripen after pollination. Peanut oil is used for cooking and in the manufacture of margarine and soap. Peanuts show up in soups and curries, and the byproducts left over after extracting the oil serve as cattle and poultry feed. Both peanuts and cashews are consumed as popular snacks. Many hotels in the Caribbean serve peanuts in their bars and restaurants as snacks, especially consumed with alcoholic beverages. Snack mixes combining peanuts, spices, and seasonings may be served.

It is important when making Caribbean dishes that call for peanuts to use fresh peanuts that have been roasted at home. Normally, when cooking with peanuts in Caribbean cuisine, especially African-influenced Caribbean cuisine, the peanuts are ground into a chunky paste to make sauces. Peanut butter should not be substituted because the flavor is very different from the pastes made with whole fresh nuts, especially when raw African or Spanish peanuts are used, and also because the texture of store-bought peanut butter is very different from that of peanuts ground by hand.

MEATS

In the history of the Caribbean, fresh meat has tended to be rather expensive and not readily available, as local livestock raising is done mainly free-range. This means that the meat supply is relatively small given the population and that much meat is imported. Imported meat tends to be of lesser quality and more expensive. Therefore, cuts of meat are used more to impart flavor to dishes rather than as the centerpiece of a meal itself. Caribbean people can eat rather well from a small supply of free-range yard animals (goats, pigs, chickens) whose meat is often used for grilling. Perhaps the most frequently eaten meats in the Caribbean are goat, pork, chicken, and beef. However, a number of wild game species are also eaten.

Caribbean islanders eat a wide variety of animals. With regard to choices of fish, most Caribbean islanders have an inordinate number of species to choose from. Some of the animals eaten in the Caribbean may not be available elsewhere in the world, either because they are indigenous or because careless fishing or hunting practices have caused their extinction elsewhere. Today, most Caribbean islands have strict rules and regulations

on fishing and hunting and have even invested in structures to help reju-
venate the populations of animals whose numbers are dwindling.

Meat dishes sometimes call for cuts of meat or scraps that are left over
from the slaughtering process, recalling the days of slavery when slaves
were given the offal of meats while the slave masters and plantation owners kept the better cuts for themselves. In any case, no part of an animal
is usually wasted; the remains of cleaned fish are cooked in soups or made
into stock, animal hides are turned into leather, and the feet of certain
animals may be kept as good luck charms. These practices are part of the
Caribbean philosophy of making do. A belief in making do with whatever
is on hand, as well as a life that maintains close ties to the natural world,
creates a sensitivity to waste and prompts Caribbean households to use as
much of an animal carcass as possible.

In order to create more of a market for Caribbean meat and to renew the
Caribbean meat industry, government officials in some Caribbean countries are now building large-scale slaughterhouses compliant with global
standards. Reacting to recent health concerns about meat safety, they hope
that by adhering to international standards and meat labeling certification
programs they can begin supplying meat processed in the Caribbean to fill
the demand created by tourists in the Caribbean who would previously
consume mostly imported meats. The trend toward meat processing in
modern, industrial slaughterhouses and away from the backyard slaughter
popular in rural areas of the Caribbean entails a great loss of traditional
Caribbean foodways. The profession of the village butcher and the cultural relations between community members inherent to local slaughtering practices are at risk, and cooking practices that rely on specialty cuts
of meat or on by-products of the slaughtering process will also be greatly
affected.

Both meats and fish can be marinated in any variety of spicy mixtures
before cooking. Marinades for fish are often citrus based and cuts of meat
are usually washed in lime juice before cooking. Open-fire or charcoal
cooking is still the preferred cooking technique for both meat and fish in
many parts of the Caribbean.

Beef

Caribbean people remark on the lack of tenderness of imported beef cuts,
so imported beef is often slow-cooked, sautéed, or stir fried, rather than
grilled. Island grasslands are used for cattle raising, but the Caribbean beef
industry is not industrially developed and mostly comprises small-scale,

free-range ranches. Cattle tend to be processed by local butchers as there are still only a few large-scale abattoirs to which Caribbean cattle ranchers have access. Although Caribbean governments have shown interest in building larger-scale slaughterhouses, the beef industry in the Caribbean is still far from industrialized. For instance, there is only select use of the feedlot system, because ranchers are dependent mainly on cattle feed imported from the United States, which is costly for them. Therefore, beef is not as plentiful in the Caribbean diet as goat or chicken.

Chicken and Other Fowl

Traditionally, before there were supermarkets or refrigeration, poultry was purchased live at the market, taken home, allowed to run around the yard, and thrown leftovers and/or feed until killed for consumption. Some of these chickens were also relied upon for their eggs. Most traditional Caribbean households are not complete without a chicken or two running around on the property. Chickens can still be purchased live at markets, but fewer and fewer people buy live chickens, and more and more people buy cuts of chicken at the supermarket.

Chicken is probably the most popular meat in the Caribbean, but its use as a regular food item only dates back a few decades. Before that, both chicken and turkey were rather expensive and saved for special occasions. Caribbean people often buy or use free-range chickens; these chickens have a very flavorful meat and are low in fat. Turkey and duck are also enjoyed in many areas, but they are not consumed as often or as widely as chicken.

Fish and Seafood

Fish and seafood in the Caribbean used to be abundant and very cheap. However, today much of the best fish and seafood of the islands is reserved for the consumption of tourists. Also, the populations of many species of aquatic life have been greatly depleted in recent years as fish and seafood no longer serve the demand of just Caribbean peoples but that of tourists and of the foreign export market as well.

In some Caribbean islands, radio disc jockeys announce over the radio when a fleet of fisherman have come in with a catch, so that consumers know to go to the dock to buy the fish. Other more traditional island societies sound the conch horn to signal the return of the fishing boats and alert villagers to the catch.

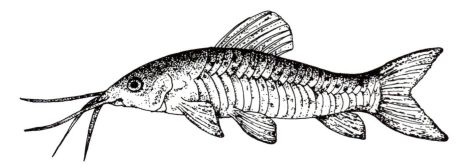

Cascadura.

Blue Marlin

Marlins have long pointed upper jawbones that look like swords. The Cayman Islands are the most popular spot for blue-marlin fishing in the Caribbean. Flesh from these fish is usually cut into steaks, seasoned, and then fried for a very short time in butter. Jamaicans consume the blue marlin most often cut into steaks and also use it like salmon by smoking it and then thinly slicing it.

Cascadura

The cascadura is a primitive armored catfish, with extremely hard scales, originally eaten by East Indians in Trinidad, and now eaten all over the Caribbean. However, this fish is sometimes hard to find outside of Trinidad and Tobago. Farm-raised catfish may be substituted for cascadura if it is not available. A classic way to prepare this favorite Trinidadian fish is to make a curry with it. The meat is also popular in other kinds of stew. Cascadura can be cooked in their own shells, or scaled and cleaned and used as fillets. To completely scale them, they must be steamed a few minutes. According to a legend cited in Alistair Macmillan's *History of the West Indies*, and made popular by Trinidadian writer Samuel Selvon's novel *Those Who Eat The Cascadura*, if someone eats the cascadura, he will always return to Trinidad.

Chip Chip

Chip-chips are tiny clams. In Trinidad, these mollusks are made into a chowder based not on cream or tomatoes, but on chicken stock. V. S.

Naipaul, a writer from Trinidad, describes the life and activities of those who live by the collection of such seafood in his book called *The Chip-Chip Gatherers*.

Conch

The conch, also known as *lambi* or sea snail, is a large mollusk found in the Caribbean. In Jamaica, the shell of the conch is called *abeng*, a word borrowed from the Ghanaian Ashanti culture. Its shell is historically significant because it was used as a horn to announce slave revolts, among other things. Indigenous peoples in the Caribbean mixed pieces of conch shells in with pottery and made hammers, cups, and dishes with them, as well as used them for decorative items like jewelry. Early settlers made mortar from a lime achieved by burning conch shells and adding sand and water. Conch have tough meat and need to be well tenderized before cooking. Conch fritters in the Bahamas are known as cracked conch; in this dish, conch is dipped into a batter made from cracker crumbs and then fried and served with a spicy dip. Conch is very abundant in the Bahamas, and conch fritters are available at almost every dining establishment and street stand. Conch is now an endangered species in some other areas of the Caribbean and is raised in farms.

Flying Fish

Flying fish is a smaller fish with a lot of bones. They are most frequently prepared whole and usually fried. These fish are so abundant around Barbados that the island is known as the land of the flying fish. Fresh flying fish are available in local Bajan markets usually between December and June.

Grouper

The meat of a grouper fish is one of the sweetest fish meats available in the Caribbean and is always a special treat on Caribbean tables. They are readily found at fish markets and are more often caught by spearfishing or pot fishing. Grouper live on the sea floor in shallow to mid-range coral reefs. There are a number of types of grouper that exist in the Caribbean; some can reach up to eight feet in length, but most are typically one to three feet long.

In Caribbean cooking, grouper are prepared in a number of ways. Smudder grouper is a baked grouper dish. Fillets are seasoned with hot pepper, and lime juice is poured over them before they are covered with onions, green peppers, tomatoes, and thyme, and baked. This dish would be eaten with white rice and a salad. Another favorite way of preparing grouper fillets is by grilling them.

Fried Fish Fillets

- small fish fillets
- lime or lemon juice
- onions (chopped finely)
- salad dressing, such as ranch or catalina (optional)
- hot pepper sauce
- Worcestershire sauce
- butter, melted
- salt
- seasoned bread crumbs (or a commercially-prepared, seasoned, dry Fish Fry coating)
- vegetable oil

Wash the fish. Combine lime or lemon juice, onions, salad dressing (optional), hot pepper sauce, Worcestershire sauce, melted butter, and salt in a bowl, using proportions according to taste. Marinate fish in this mixture for about 2 hours in refrigerator. Remove fish from marinade and drain, but do not wash.

Fill a pot (preferably cast iron) with enough oil to cover fillets completely. Heat oil in skillet until it sizzles. To test if oil is hot enough, drop a small morsel of breadcrumbs into oil. If it sizzles and forms bubbles around the morsel of bread crumbs, then it is ready.

Place bread crumbs or seasoning mixture in a plastic container with a tight-fitting lid. Put about 4–6 fish fillets into seasoning container, place lid on, and shake until fish pieces are coated. Remove coated fish and repeat with remaining pieces.

Deep-fry fish in hot oil. Drain on paper towels and serve hot with your favorite condiments. Try sprinkling them with some ground lemon pepper.

Jack

Jack is a large saltwater fish abundant in Caribbean waters. It is a family of fish that includes over 200 species, like yellowtail, green jack, burn fin, black jack, and amberjack. In French, it is known as *carangue crevalle, cre-*

valle, or *corcovado* (in French Creole), and in Spanish, *cavala*. Tuna and swordfish can be substituted for jack in recipes.

Salt Fish

Salt fish is actually dried, salted pieces of any variety of fish, although the most popular is cod (pollock or haddock could also be used). Before refrigeration, salting or pickling were means of preserving food. These are pieces of fresh cod that have been dried and encrusted in salt for preservation. In the Spanish-speaking Caribbean salt fish is called *bacalao*, and in the French-speaking Caribbean, it is called *morue*. Salt fish is combined with ackee to make the Jamaican national dish. It is combined with ducana, a type of steamed sweet potato and coconut-steamed pudding, to make the national dish of Antigua. In the Caribbean good quality salt cod is sold on trays by the slab. As salt cod sits, it gets yellow and loses its flavor, so whiter slabs are preferable. After soaking it overnight and deboning it, Caribbean cooks prepare the fish by poaching or sautéing it, or by grinding the fish up, combining it with flour, and frying it to make fritters. Salt cod is also sold in cans; in this form it requires no soaking.

Tilapia

Tilapia is a tropical fish. Its flavorful meat resembles that of the saltwater fish red snapper. Jamaicans cultivate and harvest red tilapia in freshwater ponds and then export them to countries in Europe where they have become a delicacy. The meat is prepared in fillets, seasoned, and then baked or broiled.

Goat

Goat meat is very popular in Jamaica, due to the influx of East Indian immigrants who, when they arrived in the Caribbean, began using goat as a substitute for the lamb they had been accustomed to in their curry dishes. Many Caribbean peoples of East Indian heritage still prefer goat to lamb even now that they can obtain lamb more easily. While goat meat is popular in the rest of the Caribbean, it is served most often as a special-occasion meat, and not as part of the everyday diet. Goat has normally been considered a meat for the lower classes. However, it is coming into favor with the upper classes because of its flavor, as wild game is used less in the Caribbean diet, and as imported meats, which are normally grain-fed and less flavorful than free-range, are relied upon more regularly.

Mountain Chicken (Crapaud)

In Dominica, a meat called mountain chicken is consumed regularly. The name is a misnomer, however, as the meat is not from fowl. Dominican mountain chicken is really a species of toad, known as *crapaud*, from the French. The meat is considered a delicacy and is the basis of many traditional Dominican dishes. Many Dominican families even catch their own.

Pork

Pork is extremely popular in the Caribbean and is one of the meats frequently jerked (meaning prepared by applying a spicy seasoning mixture to the meat and then grilling it). The Caribbean tradition of pork consumption goes back to the preparation of wild pigs hunted by the Amerindians in the area. The meat from the head and feet of the pig is used to make the popular dish souse. Muslim and Jewish peoples of the Caribbean do not eat pork and/or beef and instead choose from favorite meats like mutton, goat, and chicken.

DAIRY

There are not many dairy products used regularly in Caribbean cooking. Instead of the milk from cows used in other parts of the world, coconut milk is used in the Caribbean to thicken recipes or as a base for creamy dishes. Immigrants from India brought with them water buffalo and humped cattle to use these animals for milk as a way to make the standard dairy ingredients for their style of cooking: yogurt and ghee (clarified butter). However, milk did not really become a part of the Caribbean diet until refrigeration became available in homes. Not many cattle are kept on the islands for milk, and, until recently, canned milk, like sweetened condensed milk and evaporated milk, have been the preferred milk substitutes.

The Dutch-influenced islands of the Caribbean incorporate imported Dutch cheeses like Edam and Gouda in their cooking. In fact, most of the cheeses available in the Caribbean are Dutch, although there is a Jamaican variety of cheddar. The famous Dutch Caribbean specialty cheese dish, *kesi yena*, is similar to the South American dish *queso relleno*, or cheese stuffed with a meat filling.

Besides the standard Dutch cheeses, *queso blanco* is used in Caribbean cooking. It is a fresh cheese, also known to Mexican cuisine and that of the southwestern United States, and can be cooked or used in salads or stews. Its texture has been compared to tofu. Although there are a significant number of goats raised in the Caribbean, they are raised mainly for their meat, and there is little use of goat cheese in Caribbean cuisine.

FOOD PURCHASING

For centuries, since the early Amerindian farmers of the Caribbean, Caribbean peoples have lived close to the land, cultivating their own fresh fruits and produce, sometimes in small backyard garden plots, or buying food at farmers' markets. However, people are buying less and less at the picturesque farmers' markets and makeshift roadside stands, and more and more in supermarkets, which are being built just outside of towns to allow for parking. These supermarkets offer a greater choice of imported goods, even though at the farmers' markets, fresh, local produce is available. In Jamaica, the government has stepped in to regulate the farmers' market in hopes of saving this institution. Government officers gather the fresh produce from farms in the countryside, and bring it to town to sell at government-approved market facilities. Other islands still have a more traditional farmers' market, where anyone can bring produce or other foods for sale to a large outdoor market space. Curacao maintains a legendary fish market where boats pull up alongside the road and people can buy fresh fish and seafood directly off the boats. Despite the trend toward supermarkets, many Caribbean people grow some of their own food and also buy from neighbors who might set up stands in their front yards to sell produce fresh from their gardens. Many of the herbs used in Caribbean dishes and also for other medicinal or religious purposes are still bought from local herb specialists.

Markets are often social gathering places to gossip or share news. The people who sell wares at these markets, often women, are called higglers. In the recent past, there were many itinerant higglers throughout the Caribbean who would walk around selling their wares door to door. Now, however, in most parts of the Caribbean higglers are established in stalls at markets. Frequently, they ask higher prices than the supermarkets, but

Saturday market in St. John's, Antigua. © Art Directors and TRIP/Bob Turner.

their produce is fresh and locally grown and often of better quality than the produce from supermarkets. Many higglers grow some of their own produce, but they also act as middlemen for farmers in the country. Customer relations is important in the open market setting; many higglers also give customers a taste before the customer makes a purchase, or they throw in an extra item for every dozen purchased. This practice is called brawta.

As mentioned in Chapter 1, Caribbean grocery stores are now common wherever large numbers of Caribbean people have settled, such as New York City, London, major cities in Canada, and so on. These stores are unique facets of global living, catering to eager tourists returned home and exiled Caribbean nationals alike, and most of these stores reproduce some of the positive aspects of the farmers' market: direct contact with someone knowledgeable about the food and its preparation, and the stimulation of local economies and of agricultural production in areas of the Caribbean because of market demand. Although many Caribbean cooking enthusiasts may be tempted to order ingredients and items online, local grocery stores and markets outside of the Caribbean that carry Caribbean foods need support from cooks and can function as valuable places of information gathering and social interaction with others familiar with and enthusiastic about Caribbean food and culture.

BEVERAGES

Coffee, Tea, and Liquors

Coffee originally comes from Arabia and Ethiopia. The name coffee is derived from the Arabic word for stimulating drink. Coffee can be divided into two main types, one more highly caffeinated than the other—*coffee arabica* and *coffee robusta, robusta* being the more caffeinated. However, it is *arabica* coffee that has made Jamaica's Blue Mountain region, in Surrey County on the eastern part of the island, famous for its coffee production. This famous coffee, which is exported all over the world, is also used to make Jamaica's coffee-flavored liqueur Tia Maria. In Martinique, people regularly drink their coffee with coconut milk.

Besides regular consumption of coffee, tea is also consumed regularly in the Caribbean with the main meals of the day and in between with snacks. Formal afternoon high tea in the British tradition is still a grand occasion among the upper classes of the British Caribbean.

Other typical Caribbean drinks include hot and cold chocolate drinks, provided to children regularly, and Curacao liquor, an alcoholic beverage used in cocktails which is made from an oil in the peel of the Seville orange and produced near the city of Willemstad on the island of Curacao.

Rum

The molasses left over from the process of making sugar is used to make rum in many areas of the Caribbean. Other areas, like Guadeloupe and Martinique, use a liquid juice extracted from the sugarcane, also a byproduct in the sugar-making process, to make their rum. Water and nutrients to help it ferment are added before it is stored in vats. After fermentation, it is distilled to produce single distillation rum, a cheaper quality of rum commonly consumed in mixed drinks. Higher quality rums are redistilled. The alcohol is then stored in oak barrels for maturation of anywhere from two to more than ten years.

The name rum possibly comes from the word rumbullion, a term that implies a certain rowdiness and that was used to describe life in Barbados in the late 1600s. The name was abbreviated to rum and transferred to the alcohol that was supposed to be the cause of the rowdy behavior.

There are three different grades of rum. The popular brand Bacardi is a lighter rum, which was originally produced in Cuba but now originates from the Bahamas, Puerto Rico, and other former Spanish colonies in the

Americas. The medium quality rum is demerara, which is darker and has a higher alcohol content and comes from Barbados, Haiti, and St. Croix. The third type is a very dark rum known as Jamaican rum; it has a pungent, rich flavor.

Besides being consumed straight, used as a base to preserve fruits, and used in marinades to tenderize meats, rum is also used in many mixed drinks. The standard base used for many mixed drinks in the Caribbean is a simple cane syrup. Rum punch, made of lime-juice, cane sugar syrup, rum, and water, is one of the most popular mixed drinks in the Caribbean. The traditional recipe for mixing rum punch is one of sour, two of sweet, three of strong, and four of weak. This means that there is one serving of lime to two of the sugar syrup (made by heating one part of sugar in water, bringing it to a boil, letting it simmer for about 15 minutes, and then allowing it to cool), and three servings of rum to four servings of water (or just a glass filled with crushed ice). 'Ti punch (petit punch, or little punch) is the French Caribbean version of this drink using a French rum, like Père Labat made on Marie Galante or the Martinican brand St. James. The rum is poured into a glass of ice, a teaspoon of syrup is added, and it is served with a lime wedge. Rum punch and 'ti punch should not be confused with what is known as planter's punch. Planter's punch is a bright colored drink made by mixing rum with a variety of fruit juices and spices.

Cuba's famous rum drink is the Cuba Libre, meaning literally Free or Liberated Cuba. The drink was developed at the end of the nineteenth century when U.S. soldiers helped defend Cuba against Spain. They brought coca-cola with them and tried it mixed with the local rum. The standard recipe for one serving of this drink calls for one part rum to two parts cola and a dash of lime juice. The drink is made in a glass with ice cubes and garnished with a lime wedge.

3

Cooking

In the Caribbean, women do most of the domestic cooking, while men tend to be more involved with outdoor cooking, such as barbecuing, or with procuring food items, such as fishing or hunting. Most women learn to cook and cultivate kitchen gardens from their mothers. Learning to cook is an apprenticeship with one's mother and frequently involves advice about a woman's life and her relationships. Cooking together affords women the opportunity to talk about their lives and discuss the problems they are having. The privacy for these conversations is provided because, in traditional Caribbean architecture, the kitchen is located in a separate building in back of the main house in order to reduce the heat transferred to the main house, and also to reduce the risk of fire. The space of the kitchen is typically revered by mothers and daughters, and the connection they share with each other is celebrated along with their connection to their cultural heritage, both identities—familial and cultural—manifested in the food they cook and how they cook it.

Some Caribbean kitchens have not been modernized at all and use completely traditional methods and equipment; these kitchens might be so traditional that they are mere shacks behind the house. Some home cooking is still done over a fire, but most families cook regularly on gas or electric stoves. Other Caribbean kitchens compete with the most modern kitchens of Europe or the United States. For the most part, however, and certainly dependent on class, Caribbean kitchens have a hodgepodge of both traditional and modern equipment, reflecting the mix of traditional and modern techniques that characterize contemporary Caribbean home cooking. At its heart, Caribbean cooking is a peasant cuisine, which means that most cooks in Caribbean island homes are not precise with measurement and timing.

COOKING UTENSILS AND APPARATUS

Completely traditional cooks still use earthenware pots, such as those used by African immigrants, called *yabba*. These pots are very good for dishes that require many hours of slow cooking over a low or medium heat. Traditional cooks would also use gourds as storage containers, called calabashes. Meat and other foods would be smoked over an open fire in a basket-like container made of metal wire, called a *kreng kreng*. Although modern facilities may use motorized implements to pound corn, plantain, or yam, traditional cooks use a large wooden mortar. When Europeans came to the Caribbean, they brought containers and utensils made of metal and glass.

There is one main cooking utensil that no Caribbean cook, traditional or modern, would be without: the *baton lélé*. The *lélé* is a six-pronged wooden stick used for mixing, or as a whisk to beat or whip ingredients, like the vegetable stew, callaloo, so popular throughout the Caribbean.

Baton lélé.

The *lélé*, brought from Africa, comes in different sizes and is most often rubbed between the hands to make its prongs move back and forth. It is known by different names throughout the Caribbean; sometimes it is called a wooden mealie, a coo-coo stick, a funchi stick, or a swizzle stick. The name coo-coo stick is used in Barbados because the wooden stick is used to stir the cornmeal in their dish called coo-coo, a cooked side dish including a vegetable (like okra or breadfruit) mixed with cornmeal. The name funchi stick is also used because the utensil is used to stir a popular cornmeal dish, called funchi.

To properly prepare Caribbean dishes at home, a cook must also have a few other essential utensils on hand. A hand-held grater is necessary for grating fresh ingredients such as coconut, ginger, and fruit zest. A mortar and pestle are used for grinding fresh herbs for seasonings, marinades, and sauces. In traditional Puerto Rican cooking, called *cocina criolla*, the mortar and pestle are indispensable for making *sofrito*, a paste used to season dishes. For preparing fresh fruit juices, a juicer may be needed, and for preparing mixed drinks a blender is necessary. Cheesecloth should also be kept on hand, as Caribbean recipes often call for hot chili peppers to be tied in cheesecloth and added to a dish while cooking.

Sometimes special cooking pots are needed. For the many fried dishes in the Caribbean diet, a spatula and skillet for frying are essential. Traditionally, skillets are cast iron. In the French islands, a cooking pot is called a daubing pot. For soups, stews, or other dishes that require slow cooking, a large soup pot, kettle, or Dutch oven is necessary. Use of crockpots is not recommended because they often do not quickly achieve the level of heat necessary in the beginning preparation of Caribbean slow-cooked dishes. For some Puerto Rican dishes, such as *Filete al Caldero*, or for making rice, a special cooking pot called a *caldero*—literally a cauldron—is used. It is a round or oval heavy cast-iron or aluminum casserole with a lid used often to pot-roast meat (a Dutch oven is an appropriate substitute).

Earthenware casseroles are also a must in a Caribbean kitchen, and Caribbean vegetable dishes are best cooked in a pot that has a cover and a flat bottom with straight sides. A special griddle, called a *tawa*, is required for making *roti*, Indian bread on which Caribbean cooks serve a variety of curries, but a heavy skillet can be substituted. In Caribbean cooking, banana leaves also serve as cooking vessels as foods are steamed or cooked in them.

Traditionally, a coal pot is used for cooking outdoors in rural areas. Brought from Africa, it consists of a large, hand-thrown clay pot about eighteen inches high and ten to twelve inches in diameter with a wide, deep bowl at the top that holds the hot coals and that has holes in it going down to the bottom compartment. The holes lead to a column that forms the base of the bowl. This bottom compartment is open on one side to allow air to flow through the coals that sit in the top bowl. Cooking is done on pans placed directly on coals in the top bowl or on top of a grill placed on the sides of the bowl sitting over the coals. Excess ashes are removed by the opening in the side of the bottom compartment, which also provides a draft to make the fire very hot. More modern versions of this apparatus, since about the sixteenth century, have been made of iron.

Many otherwise modern homes still employ an iron coal pot, especially for making pepperpot and other stew dishes. These dishes require long cooking times, and when done on the coal pot the cost of fuel is reduced. However, there is yet another element to the continued use of the coal pot: the fact that the taste of food is different when cooked over this device because of their proximity to hot charcoal, which is frequently made from local plant matter and has distinctly flavored smoke.

A boxoven is a creative variation on the coal pot that is used for baking. It is a handcrafted oven made out of a wooden crate stood on its end and lined inside with tin. Wire shelves are placed in the top section of the box. The coal pot is then placed inside the box and the hot coals in

Coal pot.

the coal pot generate heat to bake the items that are on the wire shelves above it. These ovens were very popular in the early twentieth century in the Bahamas, and the exterior wood was often painted to add a touch of color to the kitchen. Baking in these ovens was tricky, because it was hard to tell when foods were done, as the door on the oven was the door of the wooden crate and swung open lengthwise like a refrigerator door. The door could not be opened frequently to check whether the food was done or the heat from the coal pot would escape. The Caribbean kitchen is not complete without a variety of utensils for cooking over fires or coals, such as trivets for resting the pots on top of the coal pot, long handles for preparation of foods over fire, or even legs on the bottom of pots to keep them above the coals.

Grilled and jerked meats, like those found in Jamaican cuisine, used to be cooked over an open fire but are now often cooked using large 50-gallon oil drums. However, gas grills and smokers can be used with very good results.

Portuguese immigrants to the Caribbean brought with them a device similar to the coal pot called a *fogón*. It is a rectangular stove made of tile or brick. At the top of the rectangle, there are shelves on which to cook, and at the bottom there is a space for the fire and coals, which are ventilated by air let in from openings at each side. Underneath the space for the fire is a separate storage compartment for charcoal. Later, *fogóns* were built into houses and in the nineteenth century, hoods were built over them to eliminate smoke through a chimney.

In some remote rural areas even today, breads and baked goods are still baked in outdoor ovens made of brick. However, these are becoming less used, because firewood in some of the areas has become scarce as forests are cut down. Sometimes even bean pods and seeds may be used as fuel for fires.

Cooking equipment in the Caribbean is often passed down through the women of the family line; therefore, many older cooking utensils and techniques are still commonly used. In some rural areas, kitchens may still have remnants of the smokeless fireplaces that were used for cooking before the use of gas and electricity. In the smokeless fireplace, the fire is prepared on one side under a stone that extends out from the wall, and the flue is located on the other side of the fire so the smoke is drawn out. After the stone is heated, cooking can begin. Coal- or wood-fired stoves may also still be used in some areas. These were typically large ranges made of cast iron, with the flue located at the back. Cooking is done on the stove's burners, and baking is done in the oven.

TECHNIQUES OF FOOD PREPARATION

Marinating

Caribbean cooks love to marinate meat in a spicy seasoning or liquid before stewing, braising, roasting, or boiling it. The technique of marinating dates back to sixteenth-century Europe when meat was tough and difficult to keep fresh. Seasoning meat with spices and herbs before cooking not only helped to add flavor but also tenderized and preserved it.

Seasoning up, as it is called in the English Caribbean, is marinating meat in a mix of dry ingredients, usually by scoring the flesh of the meat (or fish), spreading on the seasoning, and letting the meat sit for a while before cooking it (typically frying it). Although every cook has his or her own variation of "sisining" (seasoning), the mix in Barbados and the southern Caribbean usually includes onion, garlic, thyme, parsley, and chili. Most cooks make a large amount of seasoning and keep it in a jar in the refrigerator to use as needed. In Puerto Rico, their main seasoning is known as *sofrito*. Besides marinating meat, *sofrito* can be added to soups, stews, and side dishes. In the U.S. Virgin Islands, the seasoning tends to be drier and relies more heavily on salt. Two of the simplest marinade bases used throughout the Caribbean are lime juice and zest. Haitians use a marinade based on pickled Scotch bonnet peppers, a vinegar known as *pikliz*.

Souskai is a technique used in the Caribbean to marinate unripe vegetables and fruits. Inspired from French culinary tradition, the fruits and vegetables, also named *souskai*, are normally served together with appetizers. The most popular is *souskai* made from green mangoes.

Preserving

Caribbean cooks, before refrigeration was available, and even now with frequent electricity outages because of tropical storms, have developed a variety of methods for preserving foods. Fish can be salted and pickled. Meat is salted or dried. Vegetables are pickled and fruits are candied or made into jam or jelly.

Codfish that has been preserved by salting is a favorite in the islands and is known as salt fish. England regularly shipped pickled herring to their colonists in the Caribbean—the fish was pickled to survive the long boat journey—and salt fish is a favorite in many recipes throughout the Caribbean. One example is the dish Solomon Grundy or salmagundi (both bastardizations of the seventeenth-century French salad, *salmigondis*, made of chopped meat, anchovies, eggs, and vegetables). In this dish, salt fish is soaked, then marinated in a mix of vinegar, allspice, and onions, and then pieces of fish are served on toasted bread or crackers with some of the marinating sauce. Salted beef and salted pork are two other types of meats preserved by salting that are used widely in Caribbean cooking.

Escabeche is a special cooking technique for fish that may be considered a form of pickling, but it can also be a process of "cooking" raw fish or seafood in citrus juice. This latter process is what makes Mexico's dish *ceviche*, where fresh fish and seafood are marinated in lemon or lime juice and the acidity in citrus juice "cooks" the raw fish. The fish is served without any further cooking, with some herbs and spices, accompanied by some vegetables or tubers. The Caribbean dish escabeche, or escovitch, is based on the Spanish *escabeche*, from the Spanish word meaning pickled. In this case, the dish consists of fried fish that is marinated in a sauce made from vinegar, olive oil, and spices, with water, onion, salt, sugar, chayote, carrots, hot peppers, and allspice. Smaller fish are dipped in flour and fried whole and then marinated. They are left to sit in escovitch sauce overnight and may then be consumed for breakfast, as an appetizer, or as a side dish.

Use of Poisonous Foods

Caribbean peoples regularly consume foods that in some states of preparation may be poisonous. Recognizing when and what type of food is edible, as well as the steps needed to make poisonous foods edible, may be some of the most distinct Caribbean techniques of food preparation.

Ackee, a staple in the Caribbean diet, is only edible when it is exactly ripe. Eating an unripe or overripe ackee can produce a condition known as Jamaica poisoning, which can result in death. Although ackee trees exist in many other parts of the world, only Caribbean peoples consume the fresh fruit as part of their diet on a regular basis. The trees were brought to the Caribbean on slave ships from Africa. Many sources tell stories about how slaves would poison their masters by offering them unripe ackee to eat.

Cassava is also found in abundance throughout most of the Caribbean, and certain varieties of it are poisonous. Bitter cassava cannot be eaten raw because of the deadly quantities of prussic acid found in it. The indigenous peoples developed a process of washing, preparing, and cooking that extracts the acid.

Taino villages worked together in the painstaking process necessary to make their favorite bread out of the poisonous cassava. Once the cassava roots were dug up, peeled, washed, and grated, the villagers would extract the poisonous juices by use of a straining device. A woven cylindrical object hung from the ceiling with a looped rope attached at both sides. At the end of the looped rope was a heavy pole that the women would pull. As they pulled on the pole, it would stretch out the cylinder, putting pressure on the grated cassava inside it and pressing out the juices. The pulp left after this extraction process was then prepared in a variety of manners to be used in cooking or was stored wrapped in banana leaves.

COOKING METHODS

Baking

Caribbean cooking does not include much straight baking of main dishes, as in the style of a simple casserole. Most dishes require food items to first be fried or sautéed before baking. Breads, fruits, and desserts, however, are often baked.

Baked Plantain Custard Crisp

- 3 very ripe plantains (approximately 2 cups), or 4 very ripe bananas
- 3/4 c. milk
- 1/4 c. lime juice
- 1/4 c. brown sugar
- 1 tbs. butter or margarine
- 2 eggs
- 1 tsp. nutmeg
- 2 tsp. flour
- 1 tbs. spiced rum or orange juice

For Topping:
- 1/2 c. flour
- 6 tbs. sugar
- 2 tsp. cinnamon
- 2 tbs. butter

For Rum Cream Sauce:
- 3/4 c. sweetened condensed milk
- 1 tsp. vanilla

- 1-2 tbs. rum (or orange juice)
- 1 tbs. water

Mash plantains with milk and lime juice. In a separate bowl, cream sugar and butter, and then add egg and beat. To the egg mixture, add mashed plantains, nutmeg, and flour, and beat slightly. Pour batter into greased, square pan (8 or 9 inches). To make topping: mix together flour, sugar, and cinnamon in small bowl. Cut in butter until dough forms small crumbs (don't over mix). Sprinkle crumbs on top of batter. Bake at 350° for about 30 minutes, until middle is set and top is slightly browned. Remove from oven and cool, serve topped with rum cream sauce. To make sauce, heat sweetened condensed milk in saucepan with vanilla, rum, and water until slightly thickened.

Barbecuing

The indigenous Caribbean peoples hung meat and fish on racks to cook over an open fire. The word *brabacot* was used to refer to these racks, and the meat produced from this method was called *boucan*. The Spanish transcribed the former word as *barbacoa,* and many believe that it is from this word that the English word barbecue was derived. Others trace the origins of this word to the French settlers of Florida who would roast entire goats "from beard to tail," in French "de barbe en queue." Jamaicans developed their own special version of barbecue known as jerk.

In Caribbean cooking, sauce is not placed on foods before barbecuing. First, the foods are marinated, then basted with the marinade during grilling.

Boiling

Caribbean cuisine, with the exception of the British-influenced islands, does not include many boiled meats. Vegetables and tubers of all kinds, however, are usually enjoyed boiled. In the folk wisdom of Guadeloupan cooks, there is a rule that the lid goes on the pot when cooking vegetables that grow below the ground, but the lid is kept off the pot when cooking vegetables that grow above the ground.

Caramelizing

Caramelizing, a process of cooking or slightly burning sugar, can be done alone, as when sugar is cooked to make a rich base or sauce for a dessert (such as Caribbean black cake), or it can be used to cook meats. Meats are carmelized by putting sugar in a pan and almost burning it and then coating the meats in the sugar and cooking them in a pan. This is usually an initial process, before the actual lengthier cooking of the meats, either in the pan, on top of the stove, or in the oven. Caramelized meats may appear in stew dishes. This process of cooking was either developed by slaves on sugar plantations or was an adaptation of stir-frying meats in sugared sauces, a method brought by Asian immigrants. A popular Trinidadian rice dish called *pelau,* a one-pot meat and rice stew introduced by Muslim immigrants from India, uses this method. The caramelization gives the pelau its dark brown color. The brown layer that forms on the bottom of the pan is referred to as bun-bun or potcake (when it is rice that has been cooked), and many vie for this part of the dish as they enjoy its taste (similar to the burnt layer of cheese left on the bottom of a Swiss fondue pot).

White sugar is traditionally used to fry meat, as it caramelizes better. There are two main techniques. In the first technique, the cook begins with coconut oil in a pot, into which sugar is placed and heated. The secret to a good preparation of meat in sugar is not to let the sugar burn. The meat is then added to the sugar and oil mixture and fried. It is done when it is nicely browned. At this point the meat should be stirred and the pot should be covered with a tight-fitting lid. The temperature should be reduced for a few minutes, and finally the meat should be seasoned. To prepare one pound of meat in this fashion, 1/4 pint of oil and 1 ounce of sugar are needed. The other method of caramelizing meat in sugar begins with a mixture of sugar and water, which is heated while being stirred. More water is added and the mixture is boiled into a syrup. The syrup is set aside in a jar or bottle. (Syrup in bottles can also be purchased in grocery stores.) The sugar syrup is then added to the pan after the meat has been well browned in oil, and the meat is cooked only for a few minutes in the sugar mixture.

Frying

The technique of frying meat in sugar and oil is unique to Caribbean cooking. Coconut oil (or vegetable oil) is added to the pan and sugar sprinkled across the bottom. Diced meat is added and cooked until browned without letting the sugar burn.

Other Caribbean foods are fried in particular ways. For instance, *tostones* (the fried plantains of the Spanish Caribbean), are actually double fried. They are fried a first time and then pressed down and fried again. The name for the special Puerto Rican seasoning called *sofrito* comes from the Spanish verb *sofreír,* which means to fry lightly. In *sofrito,* ham and pork are fried lightly with onions, peppers, tomato paste, and herbs, and then added to dishes such as stewed beans, for flavoring.

The Spanish brought the technique of frying with them to the Caribbean. Once there, they substituted animal fat, coconut oil, and other vegetable oils for the olive oil that they had been accustomed to in Spain. With the influx of other Mediterranean peoples to the Caribbean, olive oil began to be imported regularly and is now used often for frying or for the lighter French technique of sautéing.

Jerking

Jerking is a method of seasoning, marinating, and then barbecuing pork, chicken, fish, or beef. Although wild boar was the original meat used in the dish called jerk, once pigs were domesticated in the Caribbean by the Spaniards, pork became the staple jerk meat. Originally for the Taino Indians and later for escaped slaves living in the remote Jamaican highlands (known as the Maroons), this method was a good way to preserve meat in the wild. Before barbecuing, the meat is well-seasoned with a special blend of scallions, onions, peppers, and spices—including thyme, allspice, cinnamon, nutmeg, peppers, and salt. The seasoning put on the meats can be either wet or dry, varying from a liquid marinade to a thick paste to a dry seasoning mix.

The origins of jerked meats are found in the preparation of meats by the Taino Indians, most notably their use of seasonings. African hunters, brought to the Caribbean as slaves, brought with them their style of pit-cooking meat and added greatly to the development of jerk. Since the mid-eighteenth century, when the first written accounts of jerking were recorded, the dish has come to be known as the staple of the Maroons, the runaway slaves, and subsequently, their descendants, living in communities in the mountain highlands of Jamaica. Although Maroons would wrap a marinated pig in leaves and steam it in its juices by burying it in a hole surrounded with hot stones, or grill a pig 12 to 14 hours over an outdoor fire of green wood, now jerk is often made on a barbecue grill, in the oven, or with a stove-top smoker. The Maroons have kept their method of jerk secret, using a special type of wood for their fire and a special blend of ingredients for their seasoning. Most other Jamaicans use wood from the pimento (allspice) tree for their jerk fire.

Jerk Seasoning

- 1 bunch green onions
- 3 tsp fresh thyme
- 2–3 tsp. salt

- 2–3 tsp. allspice
- 1/2 tsp. nutmeg
- 2 hot chili peppers, seeds removed
- 2–3 tsp. black pepper
- 1 tsp. brown sugar
- 1 tbs. vinegar
- juice from 1 lime
- 1/2 tsp. honey

Mix all ingredients in a food processor to make a paste. Store in a jar in the refrigerator for up to a month. Makes about 1 cup. This mixture is most often used as a marinade for meats like chicken before they are grilled over a fire made from a combination of coals and allspice wood.

Jerk Turkey

- 1 whole turkey
- 2-3 tsp. jerk seasoning
- 1/2 c. butter, melted
- 1 piece cheesecloth

If using a frozen, whole turkey, defrost it and follow packaging instructions for its preparation before cooking. Rinse turkey with water or lime juice. In a bowl, mix 2-3 teaspoons of jerk seasoning with about 1/2 cup of melted butter. Place turkey in roasting pan and baste it with some of the seasoned butter. Lay a piece of cheesecloth over the top of the turkey, with ends of cloth tucked inside roasting pan and saturate it by basting it with the rest of the butter. Cook turkey (no lid on pan) at 325 degrees, according to packaging instructions, basting turkey and cloth regularly with pan juices. During the last 1/2 to 1 hour of cooking time, remove cloth so that the top can brown. At that stage, the cooked pan juices can also be injected into the turkey meat with a meat syringe.

Jerk is often sold at roadside stands throughout Jamaica and elsewhere and is often cooked over coals contained in steel drum furnaces. The jerk capital of Jamaica is Boston Bay, where jerk is served out of smoke-filled tin sheds. There are many theories as to how jerk got its name. Some say that the name refers to the action of turning the meat over and over on the hot coals, "jerking" it. Others trace the origins to the Old English translation, "jirk," of the Spanish word describing the indigenous technique of meat preservation, *charqui*, which referred to smoking and drying meats. Still others claim that the word jerk is an English version of a Spanish bastardization of an Indian word that supposedly referred to preparation of pork in the style of the Quechua Indians of South America.

Jerk meat is traditionally served with side dishes of breadfruit, callaloo, plantains, sweet potatoes, and yams prepared in a variety of ways, or it can be served simply with a quartered grilled pineapple. Often it is accompanied by rum punch. Two trends have impacted jerk dishes in the Caribbean in the last 30 years: the more regular availability of tender beef, owing to the development of the cattle industry, and the influence of Asian cuisine on traditional Caribbean dishes. Now, jerked beef dishes are gaining in popularity and jerk recipes often resemble oriental glazed meats and rely on a spiced soy sauce marinade (often with honey and ginger) for flavor.

Poaching

Blaff is a special poaching technique for fish brought to the Caribbean by the Dutch but found also in the French Caribbean. In Martinique and Guadeloupe, the dish blaff, named after this technique, is often cooked on the beach with fresh fish such as snapper, marlin, or swordfish. The fish is marinated in lime juice for about two hours, then added to boiling water seasoned with onion, garlic, parsley, thyme, allspice, and a chili pepper. When the fish is added to the water, it makes a noise that sounds like a "blaff." The fish is then simmered for eight to ten minutes.

Reducing

Reducing is a popular cooking process in the Caribbean, in which meat (or fish) and/or vegetables are cooked in coconut milk until the sauce has thickened. These dishes are known by the names rundown, oildown, or oileen (see Chapter 2 for breadfruit rundown recipe).

Roasting

Since cooking outside can usually be done throughout the year in the Caribbean, many food items are roasted over wood fires or over coals. Roasted breadfruit, corn, green plantains, sweet potatoes, salt fish, and yams are some of the most popular roasted foods served in the Caribbean.

One of the most traditional Christmas dishes throughout the Caribbean is roast pig. Although it is often now done with modern barbecuing equipment, traditionally the pig was roasted on a spit built over a fire.

Sautéing

Sautéing is done by cooking food rapidly over high heat using a small amount of oil. After this is done, the pan is deglazed by removing the food and pouring a liquid into the pan. In Caribbean cuisine, this liquid can be wine or even juice from fruits like pineapple or mango. The cooked juice is then poured over the food when served.

Stewing

Stewing, a slow-cooking process in which foods are cooked in liquid, is used in the Caribbean to tenderize tough meats and to add flavor to bland foods. Often, in the spirit of making do, recipes require only a little bit of meat to give a full flavor to the dish. Traditionally, in making soups and stews, Caribbean cooks did not normally make stock; they just threw everything in a pot. However, today, the making of stock is another step in the cooking process.

Stir-frying

Stir-frying celebrates the influence of Asian immigrants and is relied on heavily in Trinidad and Tobago. The technique refers to frying foods in a small amount of oil rapidly at a high temperature while stirring constantly. A liquid, such as soy sauce, is usually added toward the end of cooking and the ingredients are cooked in it briefly.

4

Typical Meals

Although it is possible to speak of a generic pan-Caribbean cuisine with shared cooking ingredients and techniques, and typical dishes that have become expected in any Caribbean nation, regional differences and variations do exist. Many dishes have developed out of the specific culture and history of individual Caribbean regions. For instance, the choice of starch, vegetable, and legume eaten during a Caribbean meal is determined by the cultural influence on the Caribbean, whether by colonizer or major immigrant group (Spanish, French, Dutch, British, Chinese, Indian, or African), or on the behavior of a certain class.

This chapter offers historical explanations of the regional nature of typical Caribbean meals, as well as regional and class differences in food preparation and consumption in the contemporary Caribbean. The last section presents an in-depth discussion of typical meals divided by linguistic regions: sections include the English, Dutch, French, and Spanish Caribbean. The division of the Caribbean islands under the headings of their former colonizers is a useful way to designate the different cultural areas of the Caribbean instead of by geography, as an island's proximity to another island in geography may not fully explain cultural similarities or differences given the history of outside cultural influences on Caribbean regions, nor does geography help explain the several different layers of outside cultural influences on one island. The cultures of both colonizers and of immigrants, as well as neighboring countries, have left indelible marks on regional cultures of the Caribbean.

Typical meals in the Caribbean are based on the fresh foods available in the region. Many of the agricultural products are fruits and vegetables typical to tropical island areas: guava, mango, papaya, coconut, okra, cassava, breadfruit, and plantain. Other food products that make up the typical meals of the Caribbean areas come from the waters that surround the islands: lobster, conch, shrimp, and many varieties of fish. Caribbean meals are given their distinct flavors by two of the most important foods from the Americas: tomatoes and hot peppers. Many islanders eat the same dishes with slight variations and call the food and dishes by different names depending on linguistic variations. Meals prepared at home are made using recipes that have often been handed down through generations; however, many cooks have their own variations on standard recipes that make their dishes unique. Throughout the islands, typical weekend meals are larger and more festive than meals during the week.

Any description of typical meals in the Caribbean has to take into account the diversity of Caribbean food across regional, national, and class boundaries, as well as the influx of American and other international food products due to globalization and trade patterns that are changing the nature of the traditional Caribbean diet. However, beyond these concerns, beyond the simple matter of personal food preferences, and with the exception of the two religions practiced in the Caribbean that prohibit meat-eating—Rastafarianism and Hinduism—certain key ingredients have remained prevalent in the typical meals eaten in households in the Caribbean. Main meals, for the most part, have traditionally been based around fish or seafood, and accompanied by a starch and a vegetable or legume. Desserts are mostly based on fruits, especially coconut, and only rarely use rice. One-pot dishes such as stews and soups—into which are placed a variety of ingredients—are very common for smaller meals and common for even larger meals among the lower and lower-middle classes. The fish and seafood in typical meals of the Caribbean are gradually being replaced by meat, or served as a first course to a meat dish, as cattle raising in the Caribbean increases along with quantities of meat imports.

CLASS DIFFERENCES

The typical meals of the lower classes in the Caribbean are still affected by the legacy of the economics of slavery, when slaves—the majority of inhabitants in the Caribbean for two centuries—were rarely given meat or fresh fish. The typical meals of the lower classes are still based on starches and vegetables. They normally eat little meat, and only occasionally some fresh fish. During slavery, slaves were fed dried salt fish—still a very popular food in the Caribbean—and starchy vegetables rich in carbohydrates. Indentured servants brought from India and China also relied heavily on vegetables and starches. Besides their class status, these people had religious restrictions on certain foods, mostly meats, and consumed local vegetables as well as species of vegetables they brought with them to the Caribbean. Even now that meat is far more easy to obtain, soups, stews, and vegetable dishes still hold importance in Caribbean meals.

Salt fish is a standard meat substitute for the lower and middle classes. Its popularity was forged during slavery, as it was a cheap source of protein that did not spoil easily in the tropical heat. A mixture of vegetables and salt fish is still one of the most common dishes in the Caribbean, spanning all classes and regions. Jamaicans make salt fish with ackee; Guadeloupans serve it with the vegetable soup callaloo (taro leaves and okra); the Spanish Caribbean serves it marinated with sweet peppers, called *serenata*; and the French Caribbean makes it with hot peppers and calls it *féroce*. It is often accompanied by breadfruit, plantains—two of the most key vegetables ingredients of typical meals in the Caribbean—and some root vegetables.

For upper-class households in the Caribbean, meats such as beef and pork may be chosen over salt fish. Meat is now included more often in typical meals in Caribbean households because of meat exports from the United States and a small meat industry developed within the Caribbean. Wealthier families will, on the average, eat more like the upper classes of European colonial powers; culinary practices dating back to the colonial era still affect the regulation of behavior regarding exhibiting class status through food choices. Nowadays, in many islands, the middle classes enjoy eating out at restaurants very frequently, and people of the upper class have their own cooks at home. At one time, there were few breads gracing the tables of the rich in the Caribbean, as bread was considered more of a lower-class food; now all classes consume a large variety of breads at almost every meal.

AFRICAN INFLUENCE

Immigrant groups and their lifestyles have had a profound influence on typical meals in the Caribbean. Africans brought with them okra, callaloo, taro (dasheen), and ackee. The influence of these foods on typical meals in the Caribbean is profound: one of the most integral parts of most typical meals in the Caribbean is okra; the second is corn. Even the preparation of cornmeal dishes owes a debt to African manners of food preparation. A cornmeal dish known as funchi accompanies many fish dishes. In the Dutch Caribbean, their famous fish chowder is eaten with funchi. Cornmeal and okra are also combined with coconut milk to make coo-coo, a specialty of Barbados eaten everywhere in the African-influenced Caribbean. Mashed okra and plantains are cooked into a pudding called foo-foo. The preparation of these typical dishes eaten throughout the Caribbean was borrowed from African styles. The names of many of these dishes are African, referring to the consistency of the dishes: funchi means mush or meal and foo-foo refers to a doughy food. Duckunoo is also found throughout the Caribbean islands; it is an African dish consisting of grated sweet potatoes or other vegetables steamed in a plantain leaf (in Indian communities, dunckunoo is a dish made from plantain and okra). A spicy version of duckunoo accompanies meat or soup, but it can also be prepared with coconut, sugar, and vanilla and consumed as a dessert. In Antigua, however, the sweet version of this dish accompanies salt fish in a tomato sauce and is revered as the national dish. Although ackee also came from Africa and was brought to all the Caribbean islands, it is only consumed regularly in Jamaica, where it most often accompanies boiled, shredded salt fish that has been sautéed with garlic, onions, hot peppers, and possibly bits of bacon.

ASIAN INFLUENCES

As with the Africans, vegetables continued to be a main component to typical meals in the Caribbean when laborers from China and India were brought to Caribbean islands. Because many of them were poor and observed religious restrictions on meat, they were accustomed to having to spice and season their vegetables, but with the new array of spices and seasonings offered by the Caribbean lands, this aspect of their cooking took on a new dimension. Island markets even began carrying more exotic, imported vegetables from China. Asians also brought with them curries and chutneys as ways to flavor foods. The regular use of rice in their diets gave birth to the rice industry in the Caribbean. Indian immigrants brought with them a number of breads and even developed a thin fry bread, *roti*, which is unique to the Caribbean as, according to calypso writer Daisann McLane, it "has no equivalent in India."[1]

CLASSIC CARIBBEAN DISHES

There are certain dishes that are part of typical meals of the Caribbean, regardless of region, although the name of the dish may vary from region to region. Fritters, for instance, are common in many forms and are an all-purpose food consumed for breakfast, brunch, snack, or appetizer, or as a side dish. They may be made from vegetables, such as peas or beans, or from fish. Made from peas in the Dutch Caribbean, they are called cala, and in the French and English Caribbean they are called by their Yoruban name, akkra (or accras). They are most often made from mashed black-eyed peas, spiced with hot peppers, and then deep fried. In the Spanish Caribbean, fritters are more often made from salt fish and called *bacalaitos*. The French islands serve a variety of fish fritters as well, but they call them *acras de morue*. Anguillans enjoy fritters made from crabmeat, called *crab beignets*. The English Caribbean also has fish fritters. In Jamaica they are called stamp-and-go, or stamps, for short; their name comes from either a nautical term or from a reference to the speediness of their preparation, purchasing, and consumption, often by travelers on the go. Other variations on fritters exist on most islands, such as those made from bananas, pumpkins, or cornmeal. Fritters made from vegetables or from cornmeal most often accompany a fish or meat, whereas fritters made from fish are normally a main course and would be served with fresh vegetables and possibly a bread.

Another Caribbean classic dish is beans and rice. Each region has its variation, but whether living or traveling in the Caribbean, beans and rice are eaten in one form or another very often. If a person is wealthier, beans and rice may be just a side dish, but if a person is poorer, it may be the main dish. In the English Caribbean this dish is called rice and peas, and it is made from red kidney beans or small red beans. In Jamaica, it is always made with coconut milk. Even within regions, individual cooks may modify the dish, having their own special combination of seasonings and ingredients and adding to it ingredients such as sweet peppers, hot peppers, tomatoes, bacon, beef, onions, or chives. In the British Caribbean, both Jamaicans and Trinidadians make rice and pigeon peas, which are small yellow peas from Africa and which are called many different names in the Caribbean; congo peas or goongoo peas are two of the most popular. The beans of choice in the Spanish Caribbean are black beans. In Cuba, black beans may not be cooked with rice but served with it. If they are cooked together, the dish is known as *Moros y Cristianos* (Moors and Christians), and it is the Cuban national dish.

Rice and Peas (Jamaican Style)

- 1 c. dried, small red kidney beans, soaked overnight
- 3 c. coconut milk
- 2 garlic cloves, whole
- 3 spring onions, chopped finely
- 1 bay leaf
- 2 hot chili peppers, whole
- 1 sprig fresh thyme, chopped finely
- 1 1/2 c. uncooked long-grain rice
- water and chicken or beef stock
- small piece of salt pork (optional)
- hot pepper sauce
- 2 tsp salt
- 1/2 tbs. sugar

Drain beans and combine with coconut milk in a medium, non-stick pot. Add garlic, onions, bay, hot peppers, and thyme. Cook uncovered over medium heat until beans are soft (about 1 1/2 hours). Do not salt beans before they are cooked.

Drain beans, reserving liquid. Measure the reserved liquid and add enough water and stock (in equal proportions) to it to make a total of 3 cups of liquid. Add this liquid to the beans along with the rice and salt pork (optional).

Bring to boil uncovered, then reduce temperature and simmer for about 25 minutes with lid on loosely, allowing some steam to escape. When holes form in rice, put lid on tightly for remainder of cooking time. Remove garlic and hot peppers before serving. Serves 8–12.

In Haiti, cooks add an ingredient found only on their island, the famous Haitian black mushroom called *djon djon*. The mushroom stems are added to the water in which the rice is cooked, and then the caps are added to the rice and lima bean combination, which is named *riz djon djon*. Beans also show up, with or without rice, in many varieties of soups throughout the Caribbean.

Soups may include another classic Caribbean favorite, dumplings, which are normally baked dough. Fried dumplings or "dumplins," however, known as "bakes" in Trinidad and Jamaica (where they are also known as spinners), are served with salt cod or fried fish but can also be eaten like biscuits.

ONE-DISH MEALS

Soups are one-dish meals enjoyed throughout the Caribbean. Traditionally, a typical soup meal in the Caribbean would have consisted of a hot soup and maybe some bread to accompany it. However, because of the tropical climate, tourists normally reject hot soups for their meals. Thus, cold soups have found their way into the typical meals of the islanders, although many culinary purists reject the cold soups developed for tourists and opt for the traditional hot variety instead.

In the days of slavery and indentured servitude, workers would eat, at midday, a soup made of any vegetables and meat that could be scraped together from small gardens and their food rations, which had cooked in a large iron cauldron all morning. Caribbean islands with rich fishing cultures, such as the Bahamas, eat more soups with a fish or seafood base, whereas those islands with stronger agricultural traditions, such as Jamaica, consume soups based more on meats and vegetables. Guests in Caribbean households will likely be served the strained broth from a soup as a first course and the meat and vegetables from the soup as a main course, but normally a family might simply eat the entire soup for a main meal. Soups are very popular in the Caribbean for weekend meals because that is when people have time to make homemade stock.

Callaloo is a type of soup consumed throughout the Caribbean made from okra, salt pork, crabmeat, and callaloo greens. It has become synonymous with Caribbean cooking on an international scale, but English Caribbean cooks say that their islanders are not very fond of this dish. On the other hand, inhabitants of the French Caribbean consume it the most often.

Pepperpot, in its stew form, is one of the most popular dishes, found on virtually any Caribbean island. It is a traditional indigenous dish based on any kind of meat on hand: wild game, beef, pork, chicken, oxtail, or calf's head. It is given its distinct flavor by the ingredient cassareep, which is juice from the cassava root. In the English Caribbean, there is a pepperpot that is a soup; it can be distinguished from the stew form of pepperpot known in most other regions of the Caribbean by the presence of vegetables.

Curry, food cooked in a seasoned sauce, is another one-pot meal eaten throughout islands. This dish was brought by indentured servants from India. The sauce is made by using dry seasonings, such as *masala*, or a curry paste. Trinidad and Tobago do not necessarily have a stronghold on Caribbean curry consumption; Jamaicans, for instance, enjoy curried lamb or goat on a regular basis. The Dutch call curry *kerry* and the French call it *colombo*.

WEEKEND MEALS

Saturdays

In the British Caribbean, a typical informal Saturday dinner is made from black pudding and souse. Black pudding is a sausage traditionally made from pig's blood (today, more often made from liver instead of pig's blood), but it differs from other blood sausages around the world by including West Indian pumpkin and hot peppers in it. In Barbados, no pig's blood is included in the pudding and sweet potato is used in the filling. If a cook is making the sausage at home, the cook will follow an old superstition: while the pudding is cooking no one must talk, otherwise the pudding will burst. Souse is pickled pig's head and feet served with a sauce made from lime juice, hot peppers, cucumber, and stock. Trinidadians eat this typical Saturday midday meal with a bread made from hops. If eaten earlier in the day, for breakfast, Trinidadians eat the black pudding as a sausage with eggs and fried onions. In Martinique, the dish is called Antilles Boudin. Blood sausage, when served in the French Caribbean, is mixed with bread instead of potatoes.

In the French Caribbean, Saturday dinner usually consists of a special dumpling soup made from chicken, beef, tripe, oxtails, spicy vinegar, malanga, plantains, cassava, and spinach. In Haiti, this soup (called *bouillon haitien*) is also served at parties and wakes.

Since cattle used to be slaughtered on Friday or Saturday in most of the Caribbean and needed to be used quickly because of the heat, the traditional dish to consume on Saturdays in the Caribbean was beef soup. This soup, besides including pumpkins, is based on simmering the bones of cows to make a rich beef stock and is so often consumed on Saturday that it is also known as Saturday soup. It is normally served around noon and also traditionally served on New Year's Day in the French Caribbean. In the British Caribbean of St. Kitts and Nevis, soups purported to have aphrodisiac qualities, as well as the ability to cure hangovers, are consumed at noon or earlier on Saturday. The usual Saturday soup in St. Kitts and Nevis is goat or mannish water, also usually served to a groom before his wedding night in parts of the Caribbean. This soup is so popular on Saturdays that even street vendors sell it.

Sundays

On Sundays, because of the availability of fresh beef from the traditional slaughter on Saturdays, roasted beef is consumed, often for Sunday
dinner. The gravy served with the roast beef is given a spicy flavor by the
use of Scotch bonnet peppers and Pickapeppa sauce.

In the British Caribbean, escoveitched fish is a usual Sunday breakfast.
This dish calls for fried fish to be marinated in vinegar, allspice, onion,
and Scotch bonnet chile. Fish prepared in this manner is a marriage of the
island's African heritage in the manner of frying the fish with the island's
indigenous tradition of marinating fish in vinegar, similar to the seafood
dish *ceviche*, served throughout Latin America. In Jamaica, escoveitched
fish is most often served with fried cassava cake known as bammie.

In Jamaica, Sundays start with a large breakfast of ackee and salt fish,
or liver and onions with Johnnycakes, green bananas, bammie (a flat cassava bread), and fruit. Sunday dinner in Jamaica is a grand occasion and
is eaten in the midafternoon. In most of the Caribbean, Sunday dinner
is the largest, most important meal of the week. In the British Caribbean, Sunday dinner consists of rice and peas accompanied by two meat
choices or more, such as fricasseed chicken and spicy roast beef. Accompaniments are dishes such as fried plantains, string beans, and salad. Desserts are often puddings, cakes, or fruit salads. A family might drink soft
drinks, lemonade, and coconut water, but alcoholic beverages such as beer
and rum punch might also be consumed. Many of the Sunday dishes in
the Caribbean also double as special occasion dishes. For instance, white
beans (*Haricots blancs en sauce*) are normally cooked in the French Caribbean for Sundays, but also for special occasions such as Good Friday.

Many island communities have Sunday picnic traditions when the
weather is nice; these Sunday picnics may date back to the time of slavery
when slaves had Sunday off and would enjoy outdoor meals together. In
the Spanish Caribbean, a Sunday picnic is called a *día del campo*. The
traditional dish served is called *carne fiambre* and is a cold sausage made at
home from beef, ham, and shrimp and served with pickles and olives and
a salad with a simple oil and vinegar dressing.

In Bermuda, as Saturday nights are the time for parties, their Sunday
breakfasts are particularly elaborate and specially prepared by the man
of the household. The typical breakfast is codfish and bananas, which is
also served by restaurants on Sunday mornings. Avocados might accompany the dish, and it may be served as is or with a sauce. Beverages might

include juice, coffee, tea, or possibly an alcoholic beverage such as a rum punch or a mimosa (a mix of orange juice and champagne).

In Tobago, Harvest Sunday is a tradition of open house held during the summer months of July or August. For many Sundays in a row, a different Tobagan village will host Harvest Sunday and invite the people from other villages to join them in religious services and afterward in an all-day feast. For this feast, a village prepares typical Tobagan dishes, beginning days in advance of the party. They serve marinated chicken simmered in coconut milk, iguanas, goat curry, many kinds of wood-grilled fish, boiled ground tubers such as dasheen, cassava, yams, and sweet potato, boiled plantain, and many different kinds of cakes.

DESSERTS

Fresh fruits such as mango, coconut, pineapple, guava, and passion fruit are the standards of Caribbean desserts. Poorer households may make do with fresh fruits for snacks as well as desserts. Wealthier families may eat baked desserts such as cakes and pies on a more regular basis, but in general, cooked desserts are saved for special occasions. They may, however, be served more regularly as snacks, as part of a brunch, or at tea-time in the British Caribbean.

ENGLISH CARIBBEAN

The English Caribbean consists of Anguilla, Antigua, Barbuda, Bahamas, Barbados, the Cayman Islands, Dominica, Grenada, Grenadines, Jamaica, Montserrat, St. Kitts, Nevis, St. Lucia, St. Vincent, Trinidad and Tobago, Turks and Caicos, and the Virgin Islands (St. Croix, St. Thomas, and St. John). People in most countries in the English Caribbean get about 30 to 40 percent of their daily calories from cereals. Only about 1 to 5 percent come from the consumption of roots, with the exception of Dominicans who receive about 17 percent of their daily calories from roots, and Jamaicans, who receive 8 percent from roots. Sugars regularly account for about 15 to 20 percent, again, with Dominica being the exception with only 8. Pulses and vegetables both account for about 4 to 6 percent of daily caloric intake each. Some Caribbean people do not receive any of their daily calories from eggs, while others only receive about 1 or 2 percent.[2]

Throughout the English Caribbean there is a great diversity in habits of fruit, meat, and fish consumption. People in most countries average about 2 to 5 percent of their daily calories from fruits, but Dominica and Antigua/Barbuda average 7 and 8 percent respectively. Meat consumption ranges from 1 percent in Antigua/Barbuda to 18 percent in the Bahamas. Fish, too, ranges greatly from country to country, with people in the Bahamas, Jamaica, and Trinidad and Tobago receiving only 1 percent of their calories from fish, and those in Antigua/Barbuda receiving the most of any Caribbean country at 13 percent. People in Antiqua/Barbuda also hold the record for the most milk consumption in the Caribbean, averaging 13 percent of their daily calories from this product, whereas those in other English Caribbean countries range from about 4 to 7 percent. Oils count for just over another 10 percent of daily calories in the English Caribbean.[3]

Before about the 1970s and 1980s, at which time the British islands of the Caribbean began to adopt more modernized customs, British Caribbean islanders enjoyed typical British colonial mealtimes. A full, English breakfast was eaten by the middle and upper classes. They would return home later to their biggest meal of the day, called dinner, eaten at about midday, and then they had of traditional British teatime from 4:30 to 5 P.M. Later, they had a light meal in the evening called supper.

For the working classes, meals were different. Their morning meal was known as tea and consisted of porridge, or tea with bread and butter. They ate another meal, usually a stew with roots, beans, and pieces of salt meat or salt fish, between 10 A.M. and noon called "brekfuss," which they carried with them to work in a container. At night, the working classes ate their heaviest meal. Depending on class status, the big meal of the day would include meat or fish, and then a combination of side dishes like rice and root vegetables, coo-coo, fritters, plantain, and a salad.

The wealthier planter class enjoyed meals prepared by servants, which included meat or fish and side dishes like sweet potatoes, yams, dasheens, rice and peas, macaroni pie, plantains, sweet corn, pumpkin fritters, coleslaw, or a mixed salad of lettuce, tomatoes, and cucumbers. They had a beverage after waking up, usually a cup of coffee, chocolate, or herb infusion, all of which were called "tea." They ate a meal sometime later in the morning. At noon, a second breakfast was eaten, and later in the afternoon or evening they ate dinner. Dessert for the planters was elaborate; they normally enjoyed two or three different fresh-baked pies, cakes, or puddings at each main meal.

Today, typical weekday meals in the English Caribbean have changed based on the changing labor force and a changing class spectrum. Hearty morning and afternoon meals have still remained important. As a matter of fact, fish dishes may actually be eaten for a breakfast in Jamaica in Trinidad. A salt codfish salad called *Buljol* is very popular, as is salt fish and ackee served with roasted breadfruit.

Antigua

Local agriculture in Antigua is pursued mainly to support the hotels and resorts on the island. The highlight of the typical meal in Antigua is the Sunday morning breakfast, eaten like a brunch at about 10 A.M. Typically, these breakfasts are quite large gatherings of families, at which a salt fish and eggplant dish is normally served with a special tomato sauce accompanied by fried plantains. Many households have recently begun preparing their own salt fish instead of using the imported variety. Other typical meals include salt fish pie (a pie with a double crust made from mashed yams and filling including layered yam, salt fish, onion, tomato, and hard-boiled egg) and salt fish served with ducana (a sweetened sweet potato mash steamed in banana leaves). Antiguans enjoy the classic Caribbean dish pepperpot but make it with more vegetables than most other countries, and instead of crab meat, they use chicken, beef, or pork.

Antigua is known for its production of black pineapples, a particularly small, sweet, and juicy variety. The volcanic soil of the island is very conducive to raising this crop. Locals typically eat pickled pineapple in pepper and coriander as a side dish or pineapple pie as a dessert.

Bahamas

Crayfish was once a major export for the Bahamas; now it is raised and harvested more for local consumption. Traditional Bahamian fare includes much fish and seafood—often boiled or stewed—as the Bahamian coast is particularly rich in sea life. Fish and seafood dishes might be eaten for breakfast and would be served with johnnycakes or grits. Conch (either as fritters or cracked conch, both served with sauces as appetizers or as snacks) is popular, as is grouper. Those who are extremely fond of conch spend time at Potter's Cay under the bridge to Paradise Island, where local conch vendors gather with their fresh conch. Here they also sell conch meat mixed with lime juice, raw onion, and hot peppers; customers eat the mixture out of a plastic bag for a midmorning snack. In Nassau, women selling meals from street carts do a brisk business. Choices usually include chicken, mutton, ribs, and fried fish with potato salad or peas and rice on the side.

Barbados

Family farms in Barbados produce food for island consumption, crops such as yams, sweet potatoes, malanga, and fresh fruits, livestock (mainly sheep, pigs, and goats), and poultry. One of the most typical meals in Barbados is pudding and souse, traditionally the Sunday dinner menu. Pudding, in Barbados, is seasoned sweet potato mash steamed inside a sausage casing. The souse is a spicy mixture of pig's feet, snouts, and tails served in the marinade along with other vegetables. Flying Fish is the island's specialty; it is served lightly breaded and pan-fried, and topped with tartar sauce.

Bermuda

Bermuda is known for its particularly sweet onions, called Bermuda onions. Bermuda onions stuffed with mushrooms, breadcrumbs, crushed almonds, and spices typically accompany many weekday lunch and dinner dishes.

Cayman Islands

The diet of the Cayman Islanders relies heavily on the sea. This diet includes shark, turtle, barracuda, grouper, wahoo, and blue marlin. Green turtles—their meat, their eggs, and their shells (used to make soup)— have been extremely popular since before European settlement. To protect the species and still allow for its consumption, the Cayman Islands have established the Grand Cayman Turtle Farm, which helps to repopulate the species and which also provides the food for the turtle dishes served in the Cayman Islands. Blue marlin is another typical fish served in the Cayman Islands. For lunch or dinner, it could be fried and topped with a sauce, and served with red beans and rice, ochroes (okra), and a salad.

Dominica

Dominicans enjoy a meat that they call mountain chicken or crapaud— a species of frog abundant on the western side of the island. The average islander may eat this dish a few times a week during crapaud season.

Dominicans also enjoy the meat of an animal they call manicou, which is known elsewhere as opossum. A favorite Dominican method of preparing manicou is to first smoke it and then stew it in red wine. This meat is also eaten in Trinidad, where it is prepared in a curry.

The Agouti is another animal whose meat is still eaten in Dominica. The meat from this rodent used to be enjoyed throughout South and Central America, but it has become virtually extinct in areas outside of Dominica.

Another animal that is eaten in Dominica and that has disappeared on most other Caribbean islands because of careless hunting practices is the wild pig. Wild pig is prepared for typical meals in Dominica in much the same manner as other wild game. Roasting on a spit over a wood fire is the preferred method.

The Freshwater Lake of Dominica, located east of its capital city Roseau, near the village of Laudat, provides an abundance of crayfish. Two favorite meals are crayfish fried with ginger, garlic, and pepper served with saffron or annatto rice boiled with a stick of cinnamon, and rice boiled with coconut cream and crayfish.

A popular dessert that follows many meals in Dominica is a tart made from wild mountain strawberries, called *fwais* in Dominica. Tarts are also popularly made with a coconut filling.

Jamaica

Jamaican cuisine features many of the foods of the indigenous peoples of the island: cassava, corn, sweet potatoes, beans, callaloo, hot peppers, pimento, fish, crabs, guavas, pineapples, prickly pear, papaya, and cocoa. Spanish exploration of the island contributed important foods to Jamaican food culture: bananas, plantains, sugarcane, lemons, limes, oranges, coconuts, tamarind, ginger, date palm, pomegranate, grapes, and figs. The British brought beef, cakes and tarts, and breadfruit. Jewish settlers brought the eggplant and sesame. Finally, African slaves made dishes that are still popular today using ingredients found on the islands, as well as those they brought with them: yams, pigeon peas, okra, callaloo, corn, pumpkin, and ackee. All of these foodways and influences combine to make Jamaican food culture today one of the most popular and well-known in the Caribbean.

Many of the dishes found throughout the Caribbean islands have become associated primarily with Jamaican cuisine. The renown of some of the dishes has increased as they have become part of the standard fare of the Caribbean diaspora. The beef patty, for instance, can be found in major cities of the northeastern United States in pizzerias or in stores that carry West Indian specialty products. Tower Isle is a popular brand of frozen Jamaican beef patty. The beef patty is very similar to the pasty in England, a pastry puff dough wrapped around a spiced ground beef mixture.

Beef Patties

- 1 1/2 lbs. ground beef
- 2 1/2 tbs. vegetable oil
- 3 onions, finely chopped
- 3 green onions, finely chopped
- 2 Scotch bonnet peppers, minced
- 1/2 c. celery
- 1/2 c. red or green bell pepper, diced
- 2 garlic cloves
- 1 tsp. thyme, ground
- 1 tsp. turmeric
- 1 tsp. paprika or annatto
- 1 tsp. parsley flakes
- 2 tsp. black pepper
- dash salt
- 1 c. unseasoned bread crumbs
- 1 tbs. flour
- 1/4 c. cold water
- 1/4 c. beef broth
- dash hot pepper sauce
- pastry dough, cut into large circles of about 5 inches in diameter (recipe follows)

Preheat oven to 400°. In a large skillet, heat oil and sauté beef, onions, scallions, peppers, celery, bell pepper, and garlic until meat is browned and crumbly. Drain. Add seasonings, bread crumbs, flour, water, beef broth, and hot pepper sauce. Stir and heat about 5 minutes. Salt to taste. Cool to room temperature. Spoon one generous tbs. of filling onto each pastry circle. Moisten edges of pastry and seal them by crimping with a fork. For shiny patties, brush top with a mixture of a little water and beaten egg yolk before baking. Bake 20–30 minutes on ungreased baking sheets. Serve hot. Serves 10 to 15.

To make homemade dough: Sift together 4 cups flour, 2 teaspoons baking powder, and 1/4 teaspoon salt in bowl. Rub in 1 cup shortening and 1/2 cup cold water and mix gently until dough forms into crumbs. Roll dough into a ball and dust lightly with flour. Refrigerate the dough, wrapped in plastic, for at least an hour. On a floured surface, roll out the dough as thin as possible, about 1/8-inch thick. Cut out circles of about 5-inches. Fill and bake as directed above.

Weekday breakfasts in Jamaica for middle and upper classes normally consist of fresh fruits such as papaya with lime juice squeezed on top, or, more frequently, whatever can be bought from street vendors. For larger meals, and even sometimes for breakfast, the national dish of Jamaica, salt fish and ackee, is consumed regularly. The fish is served on a bed of white rice or of rice and beans cooked in coconut milk and topped with grated hardboiled eggs.

The coffee from one of the best coffee-producing regions in the Caribbean comes from Jamaica, in the Blue Mountains, and Jamaicans typically drink a cup of coffee with breakfast.

The most popular lunch in Jamaica is perhaps jerked pork. Other afternoon or evening meals are curried goat, mannish water, or stamp-and-go (salt fish fritters). For dessert, Jamaicans enjoy matrimony, a mixture of star apple and orange slices in cream.

Farmers in Jamaica will begin their day with a cup of "tea," which could be any hot beverage from coffee, to hot chocolate, to actual tea. Later in the morning, they usually have something quite substantial to eat, like callaloo and salt fish, ackee and salt fish accompanied by yams, breadfruit, dumplings, or green bananas. Both in rural and urban areas some of the favorite luncheon dishes are stewed peas (actually beans), curried goat, oxtail, escoveitched fish, brown stewed fish, or simply fried fish. Side dishes included rice, yams, cocos (also called taro or dasheen), and dumplings. Dinner emphasizes meats such as stewed beef, jerked meat, oxtail and beans, fish, or fricasseed chicken.

The Rastafarian movement originated in Jamaica, and their religious beliefs have influenced their food habits, creating a culinary subculture. Rastafarians do not eat meat but instead consume what is known as "ital" foods, vegetarian foods served as close to their natural, raw state as possible. They do not drink any alcohol, coffee, or soda. Usually, Rastafarian men do the cooking in the household, as opposed to the women in most other Caribbean homes. Their typical meals include, for breakfast, a fresh fruit platter served with roasted tubers, or a plantain porridge made with coconut milk; and for other mealtimes, they enjoy dishes like stews, rice and beans, hearty salads, vegetarian noodle dishes, jerked or grilled vegetables, and chopped vegetables cooked in coconut milk. Fresh fruit juices are popular at any meal.

St. Lucia

Until 1957, sugar was the principal agricultural export of St. Lucia. It has since been replaced by bananas. The traditional dish of St. Lucia is known as *metagee:* a stew made from salt beef, salt fish, green bananas, pumpkin, and coconut milk. In Guyana, the dish is made without the salt beef and by using fresh fish instead, prepared separately from the vegetables and dumplings. This dish might be known as oil-down, oileen, or rundown in Jamaica (referring to any dish made with coconut milk in which the milk is cooked down until there is just a little coconut oil in the bottom of the pan), or even *sancocho* (a similar dish from the Spanish Caribbean but with more ingredients).

For most St. Lucians, a Sunday brunch typically might be salt fish and bakes (grilled rolls). For a Sunday afternoon meal, one might eat a callaloo (flavored with salt beef) accompanied by a rice dish such as chattnee or a vegetable dish such as green pawpaw gratin, or a French Creole dish such as *pouile dudon,* a spicy chicken dish. Fresh cane juice or wine might accompany lunch. A dessert, such as banana bread, would be served later in the afternoon with tea.

Trinidad and Tobago

After Jamaica, Trinidad is the biggest of the British Caribbean islands. Trinidadians have one of the highest levels of seafood consumption in Latin America and the Caribbean, consuming almost 20 pounds annually per person. However, about 40 percent of that estimate is salted, smoked, or canned seafood.

Maracas Bay in Trinidad is a popular weekend gathering place for islanders, known for its shark-and-bake (sort of a Caribbean version of fish and chips) made by vendors along the beach. This typical Caribbean meal, taken very seriously in Trinidad, consists of shark steaks (marinated, seasoned, and then fried) put in a fried roll (called a bake) and sprinkled with Shadow Bennie sauce and hot pepper sauce.

Upper classes in Trinidad, often descendants of Spanish, French, British, Dutch, and German settlers, still eat very European-influenced meals: roast beef and Yorkshire pudding, for example. Other immigrant groups settling in Trinidad still eat authentic meals from their original cultures.

Chinese, Lebanese, and Syrian immigrants often also enjoy their cultures' typical foods, sometimes on a daily basis. Those of Chinese descent usually have a typical Chinese rice or chow mein at every meal. Chow mein made in the Caribbean uses fresh vegetables found there and does not include cornstarch, so the dish is of a different texture than that served at many Chinese restaurants around the world.

The food of Trinidad's Indian descendants, however, has become almost synonymous with Trinidadian cuisine. Curries can be found on every street corner. *Roti*, a flat grilled bread, accompanies curries in Trinidad and is used as a tool to eat the curry. Curry is often called *roti* as well. Curries can be made in a variety of ways—vegetarian (with chick peas, pumpkin, potato, dasheen leaves, etc.) or with meat (chicken, goat, shrimp, or even fish).

When a bread made on a griddle is torn to dip in curries, it is called "buss-up-shut" because it resembles torn cloth or a "burst open shirt." *Roti* breads are left whole and stuffed with a filling such as a curry, and rolled up like a burrito. When eaten with a split pea filling, known as *Dal* (the Hindu word for legume), this snack is called *Dhal Purie* (or *Dal Puri*).

DUTCH CARIBBEAN

The Dutch Caribbean, otherwise known as the Netherlands Antilles, includes the islands of Aruba, Curacao, Bonaire, Saba, St. Eustatius, and St. Maarten. These islands all offer many food items imported from Holland, such as edam and gouda cheeses, readily available in supermarkets. Dishes using these cheeses are popular in the Dutch Caribbean: cheese soup is often served as a first course, and a favorite main dish is *keshy yena coe cabarone* (shrimp-filled Edam cheese). For hearty meals on Aruba and Curacao, *sopito*, a spicy fish and coconut soup made with salt meat, is popular. This soup is a marriage of African and Dutch influences. Nuts are also consumed regularly in typical dishes of the Dutch Caribbean. Peanut soup is a favorite meal.

Because seafood is so affordable in the Netherlands Antilles, one of the popular dishes there is a fisherman's stew, a dish that is more expensive to make in other parts of the Caribbean. This stew, called *sopa di piska*, is a popular midday meal favorite, as is *stoba* (goat stew); both are accompanied by fried plantains and either a rice dish or funchi (cornmeal pudding). Another Dutch Caribbean innovation is a fish soup called blaff. While Dutch settlers in the Caribbean invented this poaching technique and the dish, it is eaten in the French Caribbean as well, where it is called *poisson en blaff*. Soups, stews, and fish dishes may all be served with a popular cornmeal and flour pancake called *pan bati*.

Four vegetables native to the region become the staples of typical meals when combined with fish and available meats: *concomber chiquito* (a small cucumber with prickly skin), *bonchi cunucu* (a type of bean), *pampuna* (a type of pumpkin), and *yambo* (a variety of okra). *Concomber chiquito* shows up unpeeled in stews. *Bonchi cunucu* is boiled for a side dish or a snack. *Pampuna* is boiled, mashed, and made into fritters, and *yambo* is boiled and served as a side dish to accompany a main course such as fish.

In Curacao, a larger meal, like the main meal eaten at noon, might begin with a soup or an appetizer like *kala* (black-eyed pea puffs). The main course might consist of *kokomber stoba* (cucumber stew) or *keshi yena* (a block of cheese stuffed with meat, as opposed to *keshy yena coe cabar-one*, shrimp-stuffed edam cheese) served with side dishes of tutu (corn-meal with black-eyed peas) or a rice dish. A favorite dish on this island is a soup made from the cactus growing native in the region. For dessert, there may be *arepita de pampuna* (pumpkin fritters) or *bolo di pan* (bread pudding).

FRENCH CARIBBEAN

The French Caribbean includes Guadeloupe, Haiti, Iles des Saints, Marie-Galante, Martinique, St. Barthélémy, and St. Martin (half of the former Dutch island St. Maarten). A total of 33 to 38 percent of the diet of the French Caribbean, like that in other countries of the Caribbean, comes from cereals. In Guadeloupe and Martinique, roots and pulses account for about 5 percent and 3 percent respectively, but Haitians eat more roots and pulses, averaging about 11 percent and 6 percent. In Martinique, more sugar is consumed on a daily basis (16 percent of daily calories) than in Guadeloupe and Haiti (10 and 14 respectively). People in French Caribbean countries get about 2 percent of their daily calories from vegetables and anywhere between 5 and 9 percent from fruits (Haiti is the highest at 9 percent). Those in Guadeloupe and Martinique consume about 10 percent of their daily calories from meats, but those in Haiti only 4 percent. People of the French Caribbean differ from other Caribbean countries in that they do not consume any significant amounts of eggs, and their intake of milk is also very low: at about 6 percent for Guadeloupe and Martinique, and only 1 percent for Haiti. Also, Haiti presents an odd statistic for the Caribbean: while Guadeloupe and Martinique both take in 3 percent of their calories from fish, Haitians do not eat it at all. While most Caribbean countries have about 3 percent of daily calories coming from alcoholic beverages, Guadeloupe and Martinique top the charts at 7 and 8 percent.[4]

One of the classic French Caribbean staple dishes is *fricassée de poulet au coco* (fricasseed chicken in coconut milk). Two of the most popular desserts are coconut custard and bread pudding.

Guadeloupe

Ile des Saintes is a dependency of Guadeloupe. There, coconut tarts, called *tourments d'amour* (love's torments), are the local specialty, enjoyed as snacks bought from street vendors or even children. Mainland specialties of Guadeloupe are turtle soup, and *maçonne* (a spicy kidney bean and rice dish).

Haiti

Haiti exports principally coffee, sugar, and essential oils. Its domestic agricultural production is based primarily on small subsistence farms that grow larger crops of corn, millet, rice, and sweet potatoes, and smaller crops of beans, pigeon peas, tubers, and other fruits and vegetables. The lower classes in Haiti live off of these foods and supplement their diet with fish and seafood. Northern Haitian cuisine, centered around Cap Haitian, is known for its use of cashew nuts.

A pork dish, called *griyo*, is the most typical main dish of Haiti. Pork shoulder cuts are marinated and then fried and served with a hot sauce called *ti-malice*. It is often accompanied by *riz et pois colles* and *bananes pesées*. Another typical Haitian meal is roasted chicken or pork served with *riz djon djon*. The djon djon mushroom is small black mushroom indigenous to northern Haiti. *Riz djon djon* is made by cooking rice in the liquid left over after cooking the mushroom stems. The mushrooms themselves are inedible. These typical meals might be followed by a dessert like *gateau de patate*, which is a sweet potato cake served with a coconut cream and rum sauce (called coquimol) on top. In addition to its French heritage, Haiti also has a significant African culinary heritage; for instance, one of Haiti's favorite side dishes, *tum tum*, is an African dish of mashed breadfruit or cornmeal.

Martinique

White sea urchins, known as sea eggs, used to be caught and eaten in many Caribbean islands, but their populations have been depleted everywhere except Martinique, where there are regulations and a set season for harvesting. Typical dishes made from sea eggs and eaten in Martinique are sea-egg ceviche and sea egg Creole. They can be eaten simply raw or roasted. Meals in Martinique often begin with a glass of 'ti punch, a sweet rum drink. Popular lunches or dinners include *crabes farcies* (crabs stuffed with seasoned breadcrumbs and baked in their shells), *boudin créole*, a variety of blood sausage, and acras (codfish fritters).

SPANISH CARIBBEAN

The Spanish Caribbean consists of Cuba, the Dominican Republic, Puerto Rico, and islands off the coast of Venezuela. The typical meals of these countries resemble Spanish and Latin American cuisine but also show the influence of African and French cultures. Spanish Caribbean lunches are followed by the siesta, an afternoon naptime. Countries in the Spanish Caribbean follow the typical patterns of food consumption for the Caribbean region: about 30 to 40 percent of daily calories come from cereals, 5 to 10 from roots, 10 to 20 from sugars, 5 to 10 from milk, 4 from pulses, and 1 percent from vegetables. However, people in the Spanish Caribbean tend to eat less fruits than other Caribbean people, and their meat and fish consumption is also relatively low.[5]

Cuba

Agriculturally, Cuba's most important crop is sugarcane, but it also has extensive cattle production. Cuba is most known, however, for the quality of its tobacco, rum, and coffee.

The Zapata Peninsula in Cuba is particularly known for its crocodile farming and provides meat for use in dishes. Crocodile stew is a delicious meal served with rice and black beans and fried plantains. Cubans also enjoy grilled crocodile served with bread and vegetables and a dipping sauce made from Worcestershire sauce, white wine, and butter.

For a typical breakfast, Cubans eat buttered toast and *café con leche* (coffee with milk). They enjoy sweets for midmorning and midafternoon snacks, like a piece of cake, pie, or an ice cream cone.

Cubans enjoy long dinners of about two to three hours, which start and end late. Evening meals are punctuated by breaks for smoking and talking. Black beans are popular and are served in one form or another at almost every meal, like the national dish *Moros y Cristianos* . As in most Spanish-speaking islands, black beans, fried plantain, rice, and cassava accompany main dishes. Popular dessert choices are custard, bread pudding, and rice pudding.

Cuba's culture changed completely in 1959 after the Cuban revolution and the subsequent coming to power of Fidel Castro. With the change in government came a move to socialism and a rationing of food supplies. Now, Cubans plan their meals around their rationing cards, and for special occasions they may buy food items off the black market. Before Castro, malnutrition and starvation were rampant; the rationing system he put into place has attempted to address this. Before, the very poor ate what was called *sopa de gallo* ("rooster soup") although it did not include poultry; it was only water with brown sugar.

Dominican Republic

Breakfast in the Dominican Republic is hearty and usually consists of boiled roots and vegetables, eggs made with onions and peppers, cheeses, breads, and a favorite sausage, longaniza. Coffee is either drunk black or with milk (*café con leche*) and is usually consumed throughout the day as well. Working-class people who do not have the time for a big breakfast at home will usually buy food from street vendors: meat patties (*pastelitos*), grilled meats, or fried plantain. Lunch is the main meal. It includes some type of meat with rice, beans, fritters, plantain, a dessert like a flan (*quesillo*), and coffee. The national dish, popular for lunch, is *chicharrón de pollo,* chicken pieces, cut into small chunks, marinated, and then fried. However, this dish is rivaled by *chicharrón de cerdo con yucca* (pork cracklings and yucca). An American influence has shortened the siesta and has also shortened the traditional long lunches of the rest of the Spanish-influenced Caribbean. Evening meals tend to be lighter, typically consisting of a hearty soup or stew (like *sancocho*) served with cassava bread.

The Dominican Republic produces much of the world's supply of canned hearts of palm, but on the island they are eaten fresh. One of the most popular side dishes in the Dominican Republic is any salad made with fresh hearts of palm.

Puerto Rico

The most prominent starchy vegetables and fruits in typical meals in Puerto Rico are sweet potatoes, cassava, tannias, yams, dasheens, plantains, and bananas, which are produced for domestic consumption. Other crops grown locally are tomatoes, pumpkins, peppers, cabbage, and pigeon peas. Tropical fruits figure heavily in the Puerto Rican diet. Pineapples are grown for export.

The Puerto Rican diet is heavily influenced by the early indigenous peoples of the Caribbean area, the Tainos, who ate mainly fruit, corn, cassava, game, and seafood. Spanish settlers further influenced the diet of the area, bringing with them beef, pork, rice, wheat, garlic, and olive oil. Later influences, from the African, English, and French, contributed further to make Puerto Rican cooking what it is today. Authentic Puerto Rican cooking is called *cocina criolla*.

In Puerto Rico, eggs are normally served for breakfast. A favorite breakfast food is the *tortilla española* (Spanish potato omelet). Hearty snacks similar to the Spanish tapas are normally served in Puerto Rico before lunch: foods such as *bacalaitos* (cod fritters), *empanadillas* (pastries filled with seafood or meat), and *surullitos* (fried cornmeal slices). Typically lunches and dinners begin with a soup course. Main dishes are seasoned with adobo or *sofrito*, two characteristic Puerto Rican seasonings. Meats are usually stewed and accompanied by rice, peas and rice, chayotes (christophenes), and plantains. Favorite national dishes include *sesos empanados* (calf brains), *rinones guisados* (calf kidneys), and *lengua rellena* (stuffed beef tongue). Alcohol normally accompanies lunches and dinners in the form of beer or a rum drink. Otherwise, fruit juice drinks are very popular as well. Dessert may be more often served at lunch than dinner because lunches tend to be more elaborate and are followed by the siesta. Frequently, desserts are based on coconut milk and are accompanied with coffee made from local beans. Bread pudding with rum or brandy sauce is enjoyed for dessert in Puerto Rico as in many other areas of the Caribbean.

Roast pig, a Taino specialty, is still enjoyed for large outdoor meals. Puerto Ricans often baste the roasting pig in a mixture of oil, annatto, and citrus juice. The pork can be served as is with *mofongo* (beef sausage and plantain balls), but the traditional sauce to serve with roasted pig is *aji-li-mojili* sauce; in this case the pork would be served with rice (or rice and pigeon peas), roasted plantains, and a fresh mixed salad. Puerto Ricans enjoy deep-fried pork fat, called *chicharrones*, as a snack.

Bread Pudding with Guava-Rum Sauce

- 1 lb. stale rolls or bread (approximately 1 loaf—remove crusts from sandwich bread)
- 3 c. milk
- 1 c. coconut milk
- 4 eggs, slightly beaten
- 1/2 tsp. salt
- 1 c. sugar
- 1 pinch nutmeg
- grayed zest of half a lime
- 1/2 tsp. ground cinnamon
- 1/4 c. crushed almonds
- 1/4 c. butter, melted

For Topping:
- 1/4 c. grated coconut (toasted)
- 6 tbs. guava jelly (or your favorite flavor)
- 2 tbs. rum (or juice/water)
- 1 tbs. water

Break the bread into small pieces in a bowl; pour milk and coconut milk over it, and stir. Soak for 20 minutes, until bread has absorbed the milk. In a separate bowl, cream sugar and butter together, then beat eggs in. Mash bread mixture thoroughly, then add egg mixture and all other ingredients to it, mixing well. Pour pudding batter into well-greased 2 1/2-quart casserole and set casserole in a larger pan. Pour 1 inch of hot water into larger pan. Bake at 350° for about 11/2 hours. Cool, then serve slices of bread pudding with guava-rum sauce and toasted coconut.

To make topping: stir jelly, rum (or juice/water), and water together in a saucepan over medium heat for a few minutes until it has the consistency of a sauce. Place grated coconut in a pan and toast over medium high heat, while stirring, until browned. To serve, spoon guava-rum sauce over bread pudding and sprinkle top with toasted coconut.

NOTES

1. Quoted in Dave Dewitt and Mary Jane Wilan, *Callaloo, Calypso and Carnival: The Cuisine of Trinidad and Tobago* (Freedom, Calif.: Crossing Press, 1993), p. 25.

2. Daily caloric intake figures from the Inter-American Institute for Cooperation on Agriculture. *Regional Overview of Food Security in Latin American and the Caribbean with a Focus On Agricultural Research, Technology Transfer and Application.* San José, Costa Rica (1991).

3. Ibid.

4. Ibid.

5. Ibid.

5

Eating Out

The history of eating out in the Caribbean is a history that features travelers and tourists primarily, as island residents tend to eat more at home. Besides the markets of the Amerindians, the first establishments to provide food and drink for sale were taverns and inns during the sixteenth and seventeenth centuries. They served seamen traveling between the Americas and Europe and welcomed new settlers arriving by boat. Punch houses (largely brothels) also served alcohol, but usually no food. Both taverns and punch houses during colonial days were concentrated around the main ports of call, catered mainly to the tastes of pirates, buccaneers, slave traders, and other seafaring men, and did the majority of their business selling alcohol (Madeira wine, liquor, beer, and rum punch). However, by the end of the seventeenth century, local businessmen were also frequenting the taverns, especially between noon and 3 P.M. when they would close down their stores for a siesta, during which they would nap in the shade or eat and drink at the tavern. In colonial times, taverns and coffee houses were reserved for male patrons only. According to a diary kept by a British merchant in Jamaica in 1688, local residents bought food outside of the home at any one of three markets open daily in Port Royal that offered local produce, meats, and imported goods for sale, and at the town bakeries that sold fresh baked goods and desserts such as cakes, tarts, and custards.[1]

Gradually, as more travelers began coming to the Caribbean, more taverns, coffee houses, and beer gardens opened, spreading along the coastline and inland, and becoming more diversified in the nature of their menus and services. By the nineteenth century, mom and pop stores were opening up and competing with general stores to sell goods to former slaves and indentured servants who were now earning wages (however small); these stores often served food in a bar or snack-counter setting. By the beginning of the twentieth century, food served at small, outdoor stands, located on roadsides or street corners, became very popular with Caribbean people, especially the working class. This trend is accounted for by a number of changing dynamics in Caribbean society: mainly, a greater use of the automobile, a faster rate of migration to the cities, and an increasing number of women in the work force. However, it was not until the second half of the twentieth century, with the development of a major tourist industry in the Caribbean, that the institution of the restaurant as we have come to know it was developed in the Caribbean.[2]

RESTAURANTS IN THE CARIBBEAN

The average Caribbean family does not eat out at restaurants regularly, as these establishments tend to be too expensive. Middle-class families, however, can usually afford to purchase foods sold by street vendors, in small snack shops, in jerk huts, or in fast food restaurants. Most restaurants with table service are frequented by tourists to the Caribbean, by foreign residents, or by a small minority of very affluent Caribbean families. Restaurants in major costal tourist areas are typically divided into those with a view of the water, which tend to have higher prices, and those without. Most Caribbean restaurant dining is outdoors, sometimes under a covered patio, and most Caribbean restaurants of any variety are respected for the high quality of their restaurant service. In the Caribbean, waiters and waitresses are instructed not to rush customers through their meals; it is customary for the customer to request the bill at the end of the meal, as it will not be brought to the table until then.

Tourism in the Caribbean had a slow beginning in the 1940s and 1950s. However, by the 1960s and early 1970s, much of the Caribbean economy was dependent on the tourist industry. To cater to the tastes of these tourists, most of whom came from the United States at first, the Caribbean culinary lexicon expanded to include hamburgers, pizza, and soft drinks. At that time, there were hotel lodging plans that typically included two meals at the hotel, where tourists were served foods from their own countries and not local foods. This is truly the beginning of Caribbean restaurant culture, as it has come to be known. After independence, Caribbean

Chef preparing food in Speyside, Tobago, restaurant kitchen. © TRIP/H. Rogers.

governments encouraged culinary competitions to promote experimentation with local goods by restaurant chefs.

There are now many gourmet restaurants in the Caribbean that offer world-class dining. It used to be the case that gourmet Caribbean restaurants would employ European-trained chefs, but this is not as true as it once was. As Caribbean food has grown in popularity around the world, restaurants, including those that cater to tourists, have started drawing from more local culinary talent. Now, there are also a number of excellent cooking schools in the Caribbean. Some even offer courses at the beginner level for tourists who are interested in a hands-on experience with Caribbean food.

Restaurants in the Caribbean have always had to rely heavily on imported goods. In some countries, most of the agricultural production on the island goes to supply tourist resorts with food; in addition, the resorts still import large quantities in order to offer foods on their menus that are familiar to tourists. The cost of importation significantly raises the prices of the food, which is why dining in a restaurant of this nature is too expensive for most families who live and work in the Caribbean.

This is not to say that all restaurants cater to tourists and serve imported goods. Nowadays, there is more of a demand for restaurants that offer tourists authentic Caribbean home-style food, and more restaurants of this nature are opening up. Many of these are still less polished-looking establishments and may even be well off the beaten path for tourists. Many restaurants have even started recruiting local island business by offering special discount packages, called dine-around programs, which allow resident consumers to buy a book of coupons entitling them to a certain number of reduced price meals at local participating restaurants.

Fast Food Establishments

The average Caribbean family finds fast food appealing because it is more affordable than food served in a restaurant with table service, and because it accommodates the busy lifestyles of the family members. However, eating fast food only accentuates some of the health problems experienced by Caribbean people. In response to this and to public health awareness campaigns, many fast food establishments have begun to offer salads and fruit as options on their menus. Some of the most popular fast food companies in the Caribbean are Kentucky Fried Chicken, McDonald's, Wendy's, Burger King, Pizza Hut, and Taco Bell. However, there are also popular Caribbean fast food companies: Cheffette is a Caribbean version of McDonald's, and Island Grill, formerly Chicken Supreme, is a Jamaican-owned company popular with Jamaicans for its fast food jerk chicken and fish.

When Caribbean nations gained independence from European colonial powers, American fast food companies stepped in to take advantage of the new market. In the case of Trinidad and Tobago, for example, within four years of gaining independence from Britain (in 1962), the first American fast food establishment had opened its doors in Port of Spain, where fast food restaurants of this sort are known as "take-away restaurants." This particular fast food franchise was a Royal Castle, offering primarily fried chicken, fried fish, hamburgers, and french fries (known as chips in the British Caribbean). This company did very well financially in the Caribbean and continues to do so. However, Royal Castle developed a practice that is not customary among fast food establishments: they served their food with a hot pepper sauce that was made from local ingredients, so some of the money they made was going back into the local economy. Kentucky Fried Chicken, a major contributor in sales of fried chicken, soon began opening up franchises in the Caribbean. As a matter of fact, the mid-1970s is known as the Kentucky Fried Chicken boom. In only a few years, KFC had opened at least 15 locations in Trinidad and Tobago alone. Royal Castle did not go out of business and has continued to prosper, despite this competition, and also despite the influx of fast food establishments specializing in hamburgers.[3]

Both franchises of international fast food companies, gourmet, and resort restaurants in the Caribbean tend to use large quantities of imported food. However, street vendors and small snack shops are more likely to use local ingredients. Restaurants using mainly imported goods tend to serve a cuisine that is not very true to authentic Caribbean cuisine but is instead often what is known as international cuisine, with added tropical touches in details like the plate and glass garnishes or the decor.

Street Food

Most Caribbean people eat outside of the home in more informal settings than the standard restaurant known in the United States. Stands or carts located in streets sell many snacks and meals consumed by Caribbean people outside the home. Historically, Caribbean governments have not been very strict about licensing and certification to sell food, so the average citizen has many options to make money through the vending of food without much hassle regarding paperwork. Housewives in the Caribbean, and other women with time in their schedules and a need for a supplemental income, sell baked goods on streets, in small cafes or bars that do not offer bakery items, at farmers' markets, in front of or out of their homes, or anywhere they are likely to make a sale. Many housewives or talented home cooks use their skill at canning and preserving to make money by selling jams, preserves, sauces, chutneys, and other items. Some of them are credited with selling excellent pepper sauces made from traditional family recipes and from very fresh, sometimes home-grown ingredients. In the operation of food kiosks, all members of a family usually help out.

Perhaps because Caribbean governments are beginning to institute a licensing system for public vending of street foods, most entrepreneurs choose a food sales strategy somewhere between informal sales of homemade foods and the official, public vending of street foods. Some prepare traditional, homemade meals, and pack them up in the back of a van or truck, usually keeping them warm by the use of something like a chafing dish. They then park alongside roads or in parking lots and distribute affordable, hot, home-cooked meals to the working class. Often, the meal consists of a main course, a side dish, and a salad. In Barbados, for instance, popular main course items offered by these lunch trucks include beef or lamb stew, fried chicken, and steamed fish, macaroni pie, yam,

Cooking outside, Los Charamicos, Dominican Republic. © TRIP/H. Rogers.

and rice and peas are favorite side dishes. Besides soft drinks, lunch vans often offer a good selection of fresh fruit juices and local drinks including coconut water.

In the Spanish Caribbean, street-food eating is often done at kiosks where consumers get a coffee along with croquetas (seafood cakes) or pastellitos (puff pastries stuffed with either meat or a fruit filling). Small stands near workplaces are where workers congregate to drink a beer and to socialize. Luncheonettes offer platters of *entremes* (cold luncheon meats served sometimes with cheese, olives, and pickles, resembling an antipasto plate) as lunches. Sandwiches are popular in Cuba as a fast lunch option. Bakeries in the Spanish Caribbean are known for offering takeout finger foods, such as the famous Cuban bocadito sandwich. Other street vendors sell snowcones made with syrups from fresh tropical fruits. These snowcones are called by various names in the Caribbean: skyjuice (in Jamaica), frio frios (in the Dominican Republic), frescos (in Haiti), snobols (in Guadeloupe), and raspados (in Puerto Rico).

Most of the consumers who frequent street vendors in the Caribbean are students or people who work in offices nearby. Frequently, regular consumers are those who hold more than one job and have no time for grocery shopping or meal preparation at home. In Jamaica, breakfast and dinner are the most important and hearty meals of the day, and these are also the mealtimes during which street vendors do their greatest business. Caribbean families tend to buy foods from vendors during festivals and during family outings; for instance, many families enjoy purchasing foods from vendors on weekend trips to the beach.

Eating in a restaurant and eating outside the home do not necessarily mean the same things in Caribbean food culture. Traditional Caribbean food is often cooked and consumed outdoors. Caribbean families enjoy consuming the food outside, whether it be food bought from a vendor or food brought with them from home to make a picnic. Also, much of Caribbean food has traditionally been prepared outside, over the coals of an open fire. Jerk, for instance, is prepared this way.

Food stands or carts can be found on streets near workplaces, businesses, and around universities, as well as on the beach, in parks, in town squares, and on almost every busy street corner in capital cities. Although some sell full meals, most sell snacks (or desserts) that can be either combined to make a full meal, eaten between meals, or eaten as appetizers. The Caribbean has a tradition of serving fried foods as appetizers. These include fried breads, fried fish or seafood, fried meat patties, or even fried bean paste. Most of these fried foods are known by the generic name acras.

Roadside food and street foods should not be confused with fast food. After all, many street foods are still fresh (like raw fruit) or home-made food items (often with local ingredients), made on the spot (not prepackaged), and not mass produced. However, more and more kiosks, especially in cities, are carrying commercially prepared, prepackaged products.

Some establishments occupy a space between the categories of restaurant and kiosk. Rum shops, for instance, typically serve as gathering places for single middle-class men who have dinner there on weekends. Roadside vendors and rum shops typically provide fresh seafood dishes. The seafood is usually served in generous portions and is prepared fried, boiled, or stewed, and accompanied by a starchy side dish or bread. Establishments that serve jerked pork in Jamaica, known as pork pits, also do not technically qualify as full-service restaurants but yet are very ingrained in Caribbean food culture as institutions of "roadside" food. Other roadside places that serve food and drink are simple stands selling fresh produce and coconut water fresh out of the shell.

Although good local cooks with business savvy have opened up restaurants with a more refined atmosphere, most guidebooks agree that, when looking for an authentic Caribbean restaurant experience, the key is to look for simple settings. Tourists should break away from resort beaches and go to local beaches frequented by islanders. There they may find huts along the road or on the beach with a few plastic tables set up. They may even find snack counters and small restaurants located right on the beach. Some beaches have rows of grills located on a pier or in a harbored area where people can cook their own meats or from which vendors can sell their grilled products. If grills are not available, enterprising islanders may bring their own and set up shop. Some make-shift beach restaurants can be found in the form of lunch trucks: trucks park at the beach and the vendor sets up a grill and a few tables for customers. Often the best choice for a restaurant at which to sample home-style Caribbean cooking with a local flavor is one with a simple setting: for instance, one with a thatched palm-frond roof, wooden plank tables, wooden benches, and no printed menu.

NOTES

1. John Taylor's diary, quoted in Richard S. Dunn, *Sugar and Slaves: The Rise of the Planter Class in the English West Indies, 1624–1713* (Chapel Hill: University of North Carolina Press, 1972), p. 185.

2. Dave Dewitt and Mary Jane Wilan, *Callaloo, Calypso and Carnival: The Cuisine of Trinidad and Tobago* (Freedom, Calif.: Crossing Press, 1993), pp. 27–28.

3. General information on street foods in developing countries obtained from Irene Tinker's *Street Foods: Urban Food and Employment in Developing Countries* (New York: Oxford University Press, 1997); specific information about Jamaican street foods from Marjorie Gardner, "Street Foods in Papine, St. Andrew, Jamaica: Their Role in the Foodservice Industry," paper presented at the PCA/ACA conference in San Antonio, April 8, 2004.

6

Special Occasions

Mie vaut vente peté ku mangé gaté.
Better to have your stomach burst than to waste good food.

—Creole proverb

Special occasions in the Caribbean are always celebrated by the preparation and consumption of special foods and the getting together of extended families and close friends. Holiday feasts in the different Caribbean islands showcase regional specialty foods. Food preparation and consumption during holidays are closely tied to religious affiliation. Also, the holidays, festivals, and celebrations of the Caribbean are still influenced by the experience of slavery, when celebrations often reflected agricultural cycles. Because of the close relationship to agriculture in the Caribbean, celebrations are still held in honor of harvest time, and in connection with hunting and fishing seasons.

HOLIDAYS

During the period of slavery in the Caribbean, many holidays and special occasions were celebrated by making a "cook-up," a meat dish prepared, transported, and served in a large iron pot. For example, Sunday was a free day for the slaves and while many of them would go to market to sell the produce they had cultivated in their kitchen gardens, others might go to the beach or elsewhere for a picnic with a cook-up. Many festive occasions in the Caribbean, if they involve the preparation of special foods, are still called cook-ups.

During slavery, there were four seasonal holidays in the Caribbean: Christmas, Easter (also known as Pickanny Christmas), Crop Over Festival, and the Yam Festival. Although the Yam Festival is no longer celebrated, the other three holidays are grand occasions in the Caribbean today.

Crop Over Festival

The Crop Over Festival started as a celebration of the end of the sugarcane season. The harvest season was a particularly festive occasion for slaves because they were given larger rations of food, and many seasonal fresh fruits and vegetables were available. They were allowed to freely consume the liquid from the canes as well as byproducts of the sugarmaking process, all of which promoted better nutritional health.[1] Revived in 1974, it is again quite a festive occasion in Barbados, for instance, and runs usually about three weeks from mid-July to the first week of August, often including plantation fairs, parades, and music. Today, Barbados hosts Crop Over festivities from the first Sunday in July to the first Monday in August, with the last week being the most festive. The festival begins with the ceremonial delivery of the last sugarcanes. The man and woman who cut the most cane that year are dubbed King and Queen of the crop. There are parades, contests, craft exhibitions, flower shows, music, and lots of food. The highlight of the festival is Kadooment Day, when people set up huts along the Spring Garden Highway and sell their specialty foods and drinks. Some say the best outdoor cooking on the island can be found in these stalls. Various barbecued meats are available, such as chicken, fish, and pork chops, cooked fresh right in front of the customer. Many kinds of stews are made. The traditional pudding and souse, the favorite Bajan dish, is served in great quantities. Even Rastafarians set up stands and serve fresh, raw fruits and vegetables.

Christmas

In the eighteenth and nineteenth centuries, Christmas celebrations were held on three nonconsecutive days: Christmas Day (December 25), Boxing Day (December 26), and New Year's Day (January 1). While Christmas and New Year's may be recognized around the world, Boxing Day is a holiday with British origins: After Christmas, feudal lords and nobles would give leftover Christmas treats to their tenants and servants.

Sorrel is in bloom at this time of year, and many parts of the plant are used in various aspects of the Christmas season celebration. One of the most widespread is the sorrel drink. Like sorrel, gungo (pigeon) peas are also available fresh during this season so many holiday dishes are accompanied by the dish rice and peas. For Christmas day lunch, many Caribbean households consume local fresh fruits and vegetables. In St. Lucia, islanders bake a special Christmas yam called banja.

A traditional Christmas drink in the English-speaking islands is ginger beer, while in the French Caribbean a traditional rum drink called Schrubb (rum flavored with orange peel, sugar, and spices) is enjoyed.

Throughout the Caribbean islands, roast suckling pig is a favorite Christmas dish. Although the pig was traditionally roasted on a spit, nowadays many people prepare the pig in the oven. Some, however, make use of modern barbecue equipment for an updated variation of the traditional method. The meat itself and its preparation do not change much throughout the Caribbean, but each island varies the stuffings and sauces to accompany this dish. Upper-class households in the British Caribbean and elsewhere would surely have, in addition to a roast suckling pig, a traditional stuffed turkey and maybe even a baked ham as well. Roast suckling pig is most often eaten with boiled or roasted yams and sweet potatoes.

In St. Lucian villages, a pig or lamb is slaughtered on Christmas Eve and roasted over coals. Leftovers are preserved and saved for the next two months when poorer families may lack sufficient money for food after holiday expenses.

Other Christmas dishes vary from region to region. In Puerto Rico, as well as in Trinidad and Tobago, pastelles (steamed meat patties) are a favorite of the Christmas season. They are made like the Mexican tamale: the meat filling is placed inside a cornmeal dough and traditionally wrapped in plantain or banana leaves and steamed. The similarity of this dish to tamales and other dishes in Latin America and the Spanish Caribbean shows the influence of Spanish food culture in the English-speaking islands. Spanish Caribbean islanders make a similar dish that they call *hallacas* (meat-filled cornmeal dough placed in banana leaves and boiled) that they eat on Christmas Eve and also on Christmas day for breakfast.

The Spanish Caribbean was greatly influenced by Portuguese settlers as well. Guyana, an island in the Spanish Caribbean, is famous for a different Christmas-time dish: garlic pork, a traditional dish brought by the Portuguese. In other areas of the Caribbean, garlic pork dishes may exhibit more Chinese influence, as Chinese immigrants also brought with them their own distinct recipes for garlic pork.

Desserts for the Christmas season in the Caribbean consist of puddings, cakes, and breads, all of which usually call for alcohol, such as rum, in their preparation. Imported fruits, too, such as apples, pears, peaches, and grapes are popular treats during the Christmas season. In Jamaica, the British heritage contributes plum pudding to the list of traditional Christmas dessert dishes. However, the dish takes on a distinct Caribbean flavor with the addition of native spices and rum. Yet another alcohol-soaked Christmas favorite is found throughout the Caribbean—black cake, also known as burnt sugar cake, rum cake, Christmas cake, or fruitcake. This cake is similar to the fruitcakes served in other parts of the world. It may include raisins, prunes, currants, and other dried or preserved fruits, fruit peels, nuts, and certainly much rum. The cake may be eaten with friends and family during Christmas or it may be given as a holiday gift. Traditionally, although seldom anymore, a caramel base is made for the batter of this cake by heating sugar until it melts and turns dark brown. The fruit is put to soak in the rum in October; the cake is usually baked about a week before Christmas.

Barbados has a special dish called jug-jug, found only there and served at Christmastime (when fresh pigeon peas are available) and sometimes Easter as well. It is possible that the dish is a variation on the Scottish dish haggis and introduced to the island by Scottish immigrants, but West African equivalents of this dish are also known.

Boxing Day

In Bermuda, Boxing Day is celebrated by dancing and parades and performances by acrobats, known as gombeys, wearing elaborate masks and costumes. The word gombey comes from a Bantu word for rhythm. Bermudans enjoy a number of traditional foods on this holiday: chowder (a vegetable soup served with black rum and hot peppers pickled in sherry), Bermuda fish chowder (which is really just fish stock), cassava pie, and a dessert called sullabub (a white wine and brandy cream sauce topped with whipped cream and cherries).

Junkanoo

Junkanoo is a celebration carried over from the days of slavery when slaves were given a three-day holiday starting on Christmas. Today, Junkanoo starts on Boxing Day and runs through New Year's Day. This festival is called Masquerade in some places like Guyana, and it is sometimes spelled Jockunoo. The word *rushing* is the term used in the English Caribbean for participating in the parades. Most people out rushing, dancing, or otherwise enjoying this festival eat street food that includes Bahamian fried chicken with potato salad, conch fritters, or cracked conch with Creole dip.

New Year's Day

For New Year's Day in Haiti and in the Haitian diaspora, a pumpkin beef soup is served. It is also the usual Saturday afternoon meal in the Caribbean. It may seem strange that a soup is traditionally served then. However, Haitians do not cook much on January 1, because they are preparing for the large celebration, called Ancestor's Day, held on January 2 in honor of those who died while fighting for Haiti's independence. This celebration is the most elaborate feast of the Haitian calendar.

People in other regions in the Caribbean eat many of the same foods for New Year's as they do throughout the Christmas season. For instance, roasted suckling pig is also eaten on New Year's Day in Jamaica; islanders say that eating this dish on this day brings good luck for the next year.

Carnival

Carnival is the celebration before the Catholic Lenten period, a period characterized by a denial of indulgences (traditionally a denial of meat), so carnival is a time for partying and indulging in a lot of rich food and drink. Traditionally, festivals associated with this celebration run from Epiphany (January 6) until Ash Wednesday (6 weeks before Easter); however, different Caribbean countries hold their carnival celebrations at different times, some, like Antigua, as late as July. The Mardi Gras (Fat Tuesday) celebration that highlights this is the last day of revelry before starting the Lenten period of sacrifice, starting on Ash Wednesday. Although Carnival had a religious origin when it was introduced to the Caribbean by French settlers, it has become part of the culture of the Caribbean and has lost, for many, its religious significance.

Carnival food traditions in the French Caribbean focus on rich desserts, such as cakes, tarts, and pies. On many of the islands, sweet fritters are sold on the streets at this time of year. Other popular sweet dishes associated with this festival are crêpes stuffed with brown sugar and lime juice and *bananes flambées* (baked bananas drizzled with a flaming rum sauce). In Trinidad and Tobago, pastelles (the filled pastries also served for Christmas), pelau (a one-pot rice and meat dish), and crab back (breaded crab meat baked in its shell) are eaten. Street foods popular at this time in the English Caribbean are boiled and roasted corn, corn soup, oysters, fried chicken, shark-and-bake, salt fish, roti filled with chicken or stewed beef, vegetable fritters, and doubles (roti with a chickpea filling).

The emphasis on indulgence associated with Carnival time means that many of the foods are sweet. Coconut and honey are used to make candies and cakes. Tangy tamarind balls, made of sugar, salt, and tamarind fruit, are sold. Bulla, a ginger cake popular with children, is made using fresh ginger grown in the Caribbean. There are a number of sweet drinks as well: sorrel drink (made from sorrel flowers, water, ginger, orange juice, and sugar), sugarcane-based drinks, and coconut milk straight from the shell.

Good Friday and Easter

On the morning of Good Friday, Haitians eat herring, boiled eggs, and bread. A traditional dish served for dinner on this day is salted codfish in sauce, accompanied by root vegetables, salad, white beans, and white rice. Haitians do not eat cake on Good Friday, as this is traditionally a day of penance and denial of indulgences in remembrance of the suffering of Jesus on the cross.

In St. Lucia, Catholic traditions are most evident on Good Friday, and akwa, or fish cake, and *pain d'epices*, a thin oval biscuit, are specialties for the meal. Easter Sunday resembles Christmas Day with its church services, gift-giving, and festivities.

In Jamaica, Easter is celebrated by eating buns and cheese as snacks. Many different types of buns are baked, often decorated with raisins and currants. The buns resemble small fruitcakes and the cheese has the consistency of Velveeta.

In Barbados, after attending church services, people display brightly colored cakes, Easter eggs, and hot cross buns so that friends can compliment each other on them. Many Caribbean families hold buffet-style meals on Easter, with family and friends bringing their favorite dishes. Traditional meat dishes are made from pork, beef, chicken, or lamb. Side dishes include eddoes (a tuber also known as taro or dasheen), sweet potato pie, pickled breadfruit, macaroni pie, rice and peas, fried plantain, and pumpkin fritters. Upper-class Barbados islanders drink gin with coconut water; others have rum.

The day after Easter Sunday finds many families on picnics at parks and beaches, eating leftovers. In Guadeloupe, families head to the beach and prepare *matété de crabes* outdoors.

MUSLIM AND HINDU HOLIDAYS AND CELEBRATIONS

Trinidad, with a large population of people of Indian descent, holds many Muslim and Hindu celebrations, and to a lesser degree so do Barbados, St. Vincent, and Jamaica. Many of these holidays derive from Muslim and Hindu mythology. Divali (also Diwali), a festival commemorating the return of the exiled Lord Rama and the symbolic triumph of good over evil, is now a national holiday in Trinidad and celebrated by Hindus and non-Hindus alike. Held in October or November, Divali ends a period of fasting for the Hindu community and is a day of much feasting on Indian delicacies, especially sweets such as vermicelli noodle puddings and nut-cream fudges.

An Islamic festival that ends the Ramadan period of fasting is the Islamic new year celebration, called Eid-Ul-Fitr. After religious services, Muslim families enjoy traditional Trinidadian fare, also popular at weddings and other festivals: vegetarian curries, buss-up-shut, and dhalpurie (or dhalpourrri) roti (a flat bread filled with a curry, rolled up like a sandwich).

VOODOO RITUALS

All religions in the Caribbean use food in their festivals or celebrations, and Voodoo is no exception. Voodoo practitioners even use food as part of their rituals. When a follower asks a favor of a spirit, the practice of "Iwa," he or she will make offerings of food, like cake, or grilled corn, or even a chicken.

Griyo, also known as *griot de porc,* or *grillots,* is served in Haitian Voodoo temples, especially during Voodoo celebrations for Azaka, the god of hunting and the outdoors.

CELEBRATIONS

Weddings

Wedding celebrations in the Caribbean have now become almost indistinguishable from wedding ceremonies elsewhere in the West. However, a traditional Jamaican wedding ceremony included a feast in honor of the groom held on the night before the ceremony. At this feast, curried ram goat was served along with "dip and fall back," a salted shad dish cooked in coconut milk and accompanied by rum. Some say that the goat's testicles were also roasted and served to the groom. These foods were served to him to increase his virility for the wedding night. Today, a stew called mannish water, made of the organs and head of a goat, is often served instead. On the day of the wedding, guests eat roast pig, curried goat, and their traditional accompaniments.

In Jamaica, the wedding cakes used to be carried to the bride's house on the heads of young girls the night before the wedding, as part of the traditional Caribbean celebration. Often, Caribbean wedding cake is actually white-frosted, rum fruitcake. The dried fruits, such as raisins, currants, prunes, and cherries, are steeped in rum from the time the couple announces their engagement. The longer the dried fruits sit in the rum before being baked in the cake, the sweeter and more flavorful the cake will be.

In Bermuda, a special wedding punch is made from two kinds of rum, grenadine, angostura bitters, a sugar syrup with almond essence (called falernum), and pineapple juice. Often at Caribbean weddings, the wealth of the family is judged by the quantity of alcohol served to the guests.

Caribbean weddings tend to be rather large affairs, with 200 to 500 invited guests considered normal, but they can reach up to even 1,000 guests. The more overseas family attending the event, the more prestige the family has with local islanders.

Indian wedding celebrations in the Caribbean are often much longer affairs, with parties being held the entire week before the actual ceremony. At Hindu weddings, as in other ceremonies of this religion, offerings of food are made to Hindu gods.

Other Celebrations and Foods

In modern-day Haiti, malanga (yautia) fritters and patties with a fish or beef mixture filling are served as an appetizer at important religious celebrations like christenings, baptisms, and communions. *Griyo* (also known as *grillots* or *griots de porc*), an important pork dish at every Haitian celebration, might also be served.

Griyo

- 1 1/2 lb. boneless pork, cut into 1-inch chunks
- 1 c. lime juice
- 1/2 c. orange juice
- 1 bunch of green onions, minced
- 1 hot chili pepper, minced
- 2 cloves garlic, minced
- 1 large onion, minced
- salt and pepper
- water
- 1 tbs. vegetable oil

Wash pork pieces in lime juice. Mix together remaining ingredients, except the vegetable oil. Marinate pork in mixture for a few hours. Pour pork pieces, along with marinade, into a large pot and cover completely with water. Bring to boil over medium heat, then reduce temperature and cook, uncovered, until sauce becomes thick, about 3 1/2 hours. Remove pork pieces from sauce and drain. Heat vegetable oil in skillet. Add pork pieces and brown. Accompany with Haitian ti-malice sauce and rice. Serves 4.

Sauce Ti-malice

- 1 large onion, finely chopped
- 1/2 c. chives, finely chopped
- 1/2 c. lime juice
- 2 cloves garlic, finely chopped
- 1/4 c. olive oil
- 2 tsp. finely-chopped hot peppers
- 2 tsp. salt

Marinate the onions and chives in lime juice for about 1 hour. Mix with other ingredients and bring to a boil in a saucepan. Allow to cool. Refrigerate in glass jars.

In Carriacou, smoked foods—like smoked wild goat, manicou, and tattoo—are preferred at festive occasions. Sometimes even seasoned, stewed rodent or armadillo will be served for celebrations. Curried goat was brought to the Caribbean by East Indian immigrants and has become standard celebration fare throughout the islands.

The influx of Chinese immigrants into the Caribbean has led to the celebration of traditional Chinese holidays in places such as Trinidad. Double ten, for instance, the tenth day of the tenth month of the Chinese year, is an important celebration. Sometimes Trinidadians will prepare red meat, duck, or shrimp in the southern Chinese style, or often they rely on the standard Caribbean party dish, roast pork.

FESTIVALS

Bermuda Day Parade and Sailing Races

The Bermuda Day festival comes at the end of Bermuda's "Heritage Month" in May and celebrates the beginning of summer. Like Carnival, there are parades, music, dancing, and competitions, especially the sailboat races. Families often bring picnics to this celebration, and street vendors abound. The favorite dish of this celebration is Hopping John, made of salt pork and black-eyed peas in a tomato paste. This is also a popular dish for New Year's Day; if eaten on the first day of the year, islanders believe they will have good luck. Other foods eaten on Bermuda Day include fish cakes, fried fish, beef and mussel pies, fresh vegetable salads, and dessert breads made from bananas or coconut.

Creole Day and Other Independence Celebrations

The last Friday of October is Creole Day (or Kweyol Day) in Dominica. This festival culminates a week-long celebration of Creole culture and Dominican independence from colonial forces. For this festival, radio stations broadcast in the Creole language, a mixture of French and English called patois. Also, people wear the traditional national costume: for women, this includes brightly colored dresses and headdresses; for men, black pants, white shirts, red cumberbund, and either madras waistcoats

or madras bands worn over the shoulder. As part of the celebration of Dominican culture, people eat traditional Dominican foods: *lamowee* (codfish), *hawansaw* (herring), and *jel cochon* (salted pork), all accompanied
by root vegetables. The specialty meats of Dominica are eaten with gusto:
mountain chicken (or crapaud, actually frog), manicou, and agouti. Islanders hold crayfish (*kwibish*) boils and serve their boiled crayfish with a
Creole dipping sauce. Conch (also called conk or lambie) is served soused
or curried. Hearty foods are eaten to strengthen and revive revelers, including soups like coconut milk stew (*sankotch coco*), fish broth with green
bananas (*braff bouyon* or *kou bouyon*), and foods like cabbage and dumplings. Numerous desserts are consumed during the festivities: the Dominican specialty tarts made from fwais (fresh, wild mountain strawberries) or
zabwico (a local variety of apricot), sugar cakes made with coconut (called
tablet), a type of French doughnut (*baignés*), and Creole gateau (a black,
rum fruitcake also known as black cake or burnt sugar cake).

Other islands celebrate their independence days and have special culinary traditions associated with these festivals. Jamaica, for instance, celebrates its independence from Britain during the first weekend in August
with a fried corn bread called festival, which is served with fried fish and
is named after the independence celebration itself.

Coffee Harvest Festival

The annual coffee harvest festival held for a few days in mid-February
in Maricao, Puerto Rico, celebrates the end of the coffee harvest season
and features art, music, a parade, demonstrations of coffee roasting and
preparation, and traditional Puerto Rican food, including free coffee and
coffee desserts. Tools and equipment from the history of coffee cultivating
are displayed.

This festival goes back to the eighteenth century when owners of haci-
endas would hold feasts for the workers after the coffee harvest. There is
even more reason to celebrate Puerto Rico's coffee industry today, as it has
recently made a comeback from its near demise in the 1960s from global
competition.

Oistins Fish Festival

Oistins is a town located on the southern coast of Barbados. Their annual fish festival in April celebrates the local fishing industry. Besides

music and dancing, many traditional Bajan foods and beverages are enjoyed: fish cakes, fried fish, pudding and souse, and Banks Beer.

La Fête des Cuisinières

This week-long festival in August at Pointe-à-Pitre, Guadeloupe, is put on by the *Cuistot Mutuel* Association, a professional organization for female master chefs in Guadeloupe, which counts over 300 members. The women chefs dress up in official costumes of their organization, which are decorated with the symbol of St. Lawrence, the grill. St. Lawrence is the patron saint of the association and was barbecued to death. They serve a large feast for the village featuring traditional foods from the region, especially the group's specialty, *crab farcies* (stuffed crabs).

Annual Conch Cracking Championship and Festival

In the conch cracking contest held on Grand Bahama Island in the fishing village of McClean's Town, contestants race against each other to remove the most conch out of the shell. In the conch-eating contest, participants vie to eat the most conch in the shortest time.

NOTE

1. Kenneth F. Kiple, *The Caribbean Slave: A Biological History* (Cambridge: Cambridge University Press, 1984), p. 92.

7

Diet and Health

Tourists traveling to the Caribbean for short periods risk little health-wise in enjoying the bounty of food and drink available and can probably limit their concerns to staying hydrated.[1] For Caribbean peoples, however, there are other risks associated with their diet.

Whereas tropical diseases such as malaria are no longer a major concern, malnutrition and its deficiency-related diseases have always plagued the Caribbean in one way or another. During the colonial era, lands were reserved for sugarcane production and very little was left for the cultivation of food crops, leaving the diet of Caribbean peoples deficient in many areas. Since then, the Caribbean has relied heavily on imported food products, which are often too costly for the working classes to afford. Thus, they experience problems related to undernourishment and nutritional deficiencies. Also, until recently, there has been a lack of education about nutrition in the Caribbean, so even when food items have been available in adequate quantities and diversity, people may not have been eating properly; without knowledge of the link between nutrition and disease, resultant health problems were often ascribed in the Caribbean psyche to supernatural forces instead of to dietary intake. All of these factors, as well as issues like the Caribbean climate, the history of the Caribbean diet, the genetic makeup of the Caribbean people, and an increasing reliance on processed foods, contribute to malnutrition.

Deficiencies of iodine and vitamin A have been curbed by the fortification of food products, but iron deficiencies still remain a problem. Other recent social factors like increased television viewing, less physical activity, more frequent snacking and social eating, and consumption of processed foods and drinks, as well as convenience foods, contribute to an opposite problem on the nutritional scale plaguing the contemporary Caribbean: obesity and obesity-related diabetes. The Caribbean, then, suffers from dietary health risks associated with both underdeveloped and overdeveloped countries: undernourishment and obesity, respectively.

The tropical climate of the Caribbean affects the nutritional value of the diet of Caribbean peoples. The heavy rainfall during certain seasons in the Caribbean causes minerals to be leached out of the soils in which crops are grown. The rain also leaches minerals out of grasses, which makes Caribbean lands unable to support a high population of livestock. Subsequently, the livestock that is raised on grass in the Caribbean tends to be poorer in nutrients than most other grass-fed livestock. However, any industrially produced livestock in the Caribbean today is fed with imported grains. The cost of most animal products (meat, eggs, milk, and so) is therefore made higher because it costs more to import feed. Due to the higher cost of these animal products, and without knowledge of alternative food sources for the nutrients they would provide, some lower-income families are at risk for deficiencies in calcium, protein, and iron.

One of the biggest concerns of diet and health in the Caribbean has typically been food security, meaning whether or not people are able to get enough foods and enough diversity in their foods to meet basic nutritional and caloric requirements. Lower-income households are the biggest risk group; for instance, peasants working small plots of land for their subsistence may only be able to produce small quantities of only a few crops. The income of farmers on bigger plots may be affected by high production and transportation costs, export price changes, and bad weather, and thus questions of food security may affect them as well. In urban areas, too, the poor may not be able to afford enough quantity of food or enough diversity of foods. Subsidies for the production of staple food crops and for increased agricultural technology have been established to combat food insecurity. Moves to sustainable agriculture—methods of agricultural production that have less of a negative impact on the environment—allow food production to put less strain on natural resources as the population in the Caribbean grows. Methods such as these would ensure adequate food production in the future.

Other factors affecting diet and health have to do with the genetic makeup of the Caribbean people. Many people of West African heritage are lactose intolerant because of the traditional lack of dairy in the West African diet. Lactose intolerance negatively affects Afro-Caribbean infants and children who may develop rickets if they are not getting required amounts of calcium and vitamin D from dairy products like milk, or from other sources, and if they are kept indoors too much (sunlight stimulates vitamin D production). However, as adults, Afro-Caribbean peoples have less calcium deficiency-related health problems than their white counterparts.[2] Afro-Caribbean people also have genetic problems related to salt retention, which can lead to hypertension. The diet of Africans traditionally did not include much salt or salted products. When African slaves were brought to the Caribbean, their salt intake increased greatly because of salted products like salt fish and salt pork. Salt retention has caused problems in the population, particularly in pregnant women, contributing to still births and infant mortality.

The diet of a slave in the Caribbean consisted typically of a large percentage of cereals, like corn or rice, regular supplies of cassava and plantains, and other produce like yams, bananas, sweet potatoes, okra, coconuts, and leafy green vegetables, as well as very small rations of salt fish, beef, or pork. However the barrel-curing process for fish and meats imported to the Caribbean from Europe for slave consumption at this time was not ideal for storage in the tropical heat on the islands. This would have meant that most of the meat and fish was rancid by the time it reached the slaves and was certainly very low in nutrients. Not only that, but the rancidity of the meat and fish would have further leached vitamin A, which was also lacking in their diets. By the end of the eighteenth century, slaves were given small plots of land to cultivate crops and raise hogs and chickens; however, a significant amount of these food items were sold for profit (to buy clothes, alcohol, and tobacco) rather than consumed. Coupled with small portions, infrequent daily meals, and the tremendous expenditure of calories from working in sugarcane fields, slaves were generally constantly undernourished and suffered from health problems related to protein deficiencies from their high-carbohydrate, low-protein diet. Legumes were given to slaves on occasion and helped to boost protein and iron intake. Iron cooking pots used by slaves to prepare meals for themselves also contributed both positively and negatively to their nutritional health. When fruits and vegetables were cooked for long periods of time in these iron pots, their vitamin C content was greatly diminished and could contribute to a vitamin C deficiency if not supplemented by the consumption of raw fruits and vegetables. However, the iron cooking pots added some iron to the foods cooked in them. Moreover, even the typical food items in the diet of slaves were not always available to them because of factors impacting the shipment of goods to the Caribbean: for instance, war, economic strife, and bad weather such as hurricanes or droughts.[3]

The iron deficiency and resulting anemia experienced by many slaves is still a problem in the Caribbean. Iron deficiency from hookworm infection is no longer as big a problem in the Caribbean as it once was, but dietary anemia is still a problem because of the lack of this nutrient in the typical foods of the Caribbean diet and the ways in which these foods are combined. For instance, vegetable sources of iron are not as easily absorbed by the body as are animal sources of iron, such as beef and fish. Iron from black beans is not easily absorbed, but when combined with a starch like rice, the iron absorption rate increases greatly. Most Caribbean regions have a favorite rice and bean dish, and thus people have developed a way to increase iron intake in their diet through effective food combinations. Young children and pregnant women are at the greatest risk for anemia.

Protein deficiencies are prevalent among groups in the Caribbean whose diet consists mainly of starches, like roots, and fruits rather than cereals. The traditional Caribbean diet relies heavily on the staples of tubers, plantains, and breadfruit, all of which have low-protein contents. The introduction of cereals into the Caribbean diet has helped to increase protein levels. The term protein-calorie malnutrition is used to discuss health problems of this type in the Caribbean, because the term adequately conveys the need for proper calorie intake along with adequate protein intake. Kwashiorkor is one form of protein malnutrition, but another form prevalent in the Caribbean, known as marasmus, is caused by a deficiency in both calories and protein.

In some Caribbean countries like Antigua/Barbuda, Barbados, the British Virgin Islands, Dominica, Guyana, and St. Lucia, obesity affects more than half of the population of adult women and more than a quarter of the men.[4] Attending the problem of obesity are deaths related to diabetes, high blood pressure, heart disease, stroke, and cancer. In the past thirty years, with increased modernization and the influx of fast food establishments, the Caribbean diet has moved from a diet that was low in calories and fat and high in fiber to one that is high in fat and refined sugar and low in fiber. Some studies have found that excess fruit juice consumption in children may lead to obesity. In lower-income families, these drinks may be given to children as a substitute for milk because they are less expensive, or as a replacement for an adequate number of daily servings of fruits and vegetables. However, many of the drinks marketed as fruit juice contain very little fruit juice and a lot of refined sugar and artificial flavoring. Physical activity has also declined due to such factors as increased mechanization of production, urbanization, improved transportation systems, and an increase in sedentary activities like watching television and playing computer games. Women may be particularly susceptible to obesity because they often get less exercise. Jobs for middle- and upper-class women in the Caribbean do not entail much physical activity, and the social psychology of the Caribbean provides few opportunities for adult women to engage in athletics. The hot climate is also a deterrent to exercise. Another factor possibly contributing to obesity is the association made between being overweight and being in good health. This belief is decreasing as a more Westernized notion of beauty is being imported to Caribbean areas and as undernourishment becomes less of a problem.

In the past, adequate medical attention for health problems may have been difficult to obtain in some Caribbean countries. Today, this is less of an obstacle to good health. However, the values and beliefs of Caribbean peoples may suggest alternatives to Western (allopathic) medicine. Caribbean people who practice one of the many folk religions may turn to spiritual leaders for their health problems, or to foods ascribed special healing properties. Many local village herbalists provide plants and instructions for their use to local residents as cures for illness. They are also a source for many of the ingredients in the "health tonics" that are essential to the Caribbean ideal of good health. These health tonics can be hot broths or soups, or they can be cold or room temperature drinks. Most often, health tonics are actually herbal rums, that is, strong undiluted cask rum in which different kinds of herbs have been left to soak for about a week. The ritual they follow is this: first they drink it by the shot but pour the last of the rum on the floor to honor the spirits and to keep bad spirits away. Then, they follow it with a glass of water that is swished around the mouth and spat out. Finally, they pour another glass of water that they drink. Popular herbal rums for common ailments are as follows: anise is good for stomach problems, as is ginger; cinnamon gets rid of cold symptoms; bois bande is an aphrodisiac and also assures good prostate health in older men; basil reduces fever; rosemary purifies the blood; hibiscus maintains good kidney health; and lapsent cures hangovers.

Another important medical personage in the Caribbean besides the herbalist is the local bush doctor. This is a continuation of the indigenous medicine practiced by the Tainos before the Europeans arrived and requires the use of local plants. The indigenous knowledge of natural healing was combined with similar African knowledge carried by the slaves who were brought to the Caribbean and who adapted their skills with medicinal plants to the local plants. This knowledge is kept secret, and only those chosen to follow the path of the bush doctor are trained. Recipes for healing potions using plants are very specific and consider numerous factors in the patient's life. Plants used for medicinal purposes can be in the form of hot tea, cold tea, herbal baths, poultices, or as a paste or oil for rubbing on the body. Plants are also used in religious rituals, as in obeah and voodoo, for healing purposes, and also kept as charms. Most people believe that general good health is ensured by a "bush bath," an herbal bath taken according to the prescriptions of the local bush doctor.

NOTES

1. Travelers to Caribbean beaches should make sure to avoid the Manchineel tree. Its sap and fruit are highly poisonous. These trees are often marked, usually with a red sign.

2. Kenneth F. Kiple, *The Caribbean Slave: A Biological History* (Cambridge: Cambridge University Press, 1984), p. 43.

3. Kiple, pp. 76–89.

4. Knox Hagley, "An Overview of the Problem" *Cajanus* 23, 1 (1990): pp. 8–13.

Glossary

Acrra   Salt fish fritters.

Adobo   In most of the Caribbean, adobo is a dry mix or paste that is used in the preparation of meats. In Cuba, it is a liquid marinade.

Agouti   Species of rodent eaten in Dominica.

Aji-li-mojili   Type of hot pepper sauce.

Arepita di pampuna   Pumpkin fritters enjoyed in the Dutch Caribbean.

Baigani   Eggplant fritter popular in East and West Indian cuisines.

Bammy   Bread made from cassava flour, also spelled bammie.

Bananes pesées   Haitian name for fried plantain chips.

Bara   Type of fry bread popular in Trinidad and Tobago.

Baton lélé   Pronged wooden stick used in cooking for stirring, mixing, and beating, also known as wooden mealie, coo-coo stick, funchi stick, and swizzle stick.

Beignets   Sweet fritters or pastries, also spelled baignés.

Bill   Tool used to cut sugarcane stalks.

Blaff   Technique of poaching fish.

Bocadito   Small sandwiches eaten in the Spanish Caribbean, especially Cuba.

Boudin créole   Blood sausage

Bouillon haitien   Type of dumpling soup popular for special occasions in Haiti.

Box oven   Oven that uses heat from a coal pot.

Brawta   In Jamaican patois, name for practice whereby grocers give a sample or a little extra of their product.

Bullas   Gingerbread cookie.

Bun-bun   Burnt part of a dish that is left at the bottom of a pot, also known as the potcake.

Buren   Taino clay griddle.

Buss-up-shut   Ripped pieces of bread served with curry.

Cafe con leche   Coffee with steamed milk.

Caldero   Larger, heavy-duty cooking pot.

Callaloo   Soup or stew made from various ingredients throughout the Caribbean.

Carne fiambre   Cold sausage dish.

Cassareep   Syrup made from boiled cassava.

Channa   Curried chickpeas.

Chapatti   Fried bread popular in East Indian cuisine.

Chicharrón de pollo   Small chunks of chicken that have been fried until crispy.

Coa   Agricultural tool used by the Amerindian peoples of the Caribbean.

Coal pot   Cooking device that allows foods to be cooked over hot coals.

Cocina criolla   Traditional cuisine of Puerto Rico.

Conuco farming   Amerindian practice of planting seeds in mounds of soil.

Coo-coo   Any side dish, but often one made from cornmeal (also cou-cou).

Cook-up   Any special occasion that involves bringing people together to eat. Typically, it meant that the food was prepared in one large pot.

Crabs farcies   Crab meat mixed with seasoning and served in its shell.

Crop Over Festival   Festivity held at the end of the sugarcane harvest.

Croquetas   Ground meat patties that are dipped in egg and bread crumbs and then fried. They can be eaten alone or put between two pieces of bread and eaten like a sandwich.

Dahl   Porridge made from lentils.

Dal   Split pea spread or dip for East Indian breads. Also, the Hindu word for legume.

Dhal purie   Dish that includes **dal** wrapped in a **roti** bread. Also, spelled dal purie.

Dip and fall back   Salt fish cooked in coconut milk, served in Jamaica for special occasions such as weddings.

Divali   Also spelled Diwali. Hindu festival that commemorates the return of Lord Rama. A national holiday in Trinidad.

Doubles   Snack made of two pieces of bara bread with curried chickpeas placed between them.

Ducana   Steamed pudding made from sweet potato and coconut, also spelled duckunoo.

Dulce de tomate   Sweet pudding made from tomatoes.

Empanadillas   Pastries filled with seafood or meat.

Escoveitch   Fried fish marinated in vinegar.

Féroce   French Caribbean name for a dish that combines hot peppers and salt fish.

Floats   Type of fried bread.

Fogón   Portuguese device built for cooking food over an open fire.

Fricasée de poulet au coco   French name for fricasseed chicken in coconut milk.

Fufu   Sticky dough that is fried in balls and served as a type of dumpling.

Funchi   Also known as funghi and fungi, a boiled cake made from cornmeal.

Gateau de patate   Sweet potato cake served with coconut cream and rum sauce.

Ghee   Clarified butter used in East Indian cuisine.

Griyo (Griots)   Haitian pork dish served at special occasions and accompanied by ti-malice sauce.

Hallacas   Cornmeal stuffed with a meat mixture and boiled in banana leaves, similar to tamales.

Higglers   Street vendors or farmers' market salespeople.

Ital   Rastafarian concept of "clean" food, vegetarian food that is normally consumed as close to its raw, natural state as possible.

Iwa   In Voodoo, the practice of making offerings to the spirits.

Jamaica poisoning   The often deadly toxic illness experienced from eating a raw ackee.

Jerk   Jamaican barbecue.

Jug-jug   Bajan corn, meat, and bean mixture similar to the Scottish dish haggis.

Junkanoo   Festival held after Christmas until New Year's.

Kadooment Day   Day during Crop Over Festival on which outdoor stands are set up along the roadside selling traditional foods.

Kalas   Dutch word for a fritter made from black-eyed peas.

Kebab   Chunks of meat grilled on skewers.

Keshy yena coe cabarone   Shrimp-stuffed cheese made in the Dutch Caribbean.

Kesi yena (or keshy yena)   Meat-stuffed cheese made in the Dutch Caribbean.

Kreng kreng   Metal basket used for smoking foods over a fire.

Kwashiorkor   Form of protein malnutrition.

Lechon asado   Roast suckling pig.

Maçonne   Spicy kidney bean and rice dish.

Manicou   Dominican word for opossum.

Mannish water   Stew made of the organs and head of a goat served to a groom before his wedding night.

Marasmus   Protein and calorie deficiency.

Masala   Seasoning mixture made from coriander, anise, cloves, cumin, fenugreek, mustard, and turmeric.

Metagee   Stew made from salt beef, salt fish, green bananas, pumpkin, and coconut milk.

Metai   Fried bread enjoyed by East Indian immigrants to the Caribbean.

Metété de crabes   Crab stew enjoyed in Guadeloupe and Martinique.

Milho frito   Specialty of Portugal consisting of fried cubes of dough.

Mofongo   Mashed, fried plantain.

Moros y cristianos   Cuban black beans and rice.

Mountain chicken   Name for a frog consumed in Dominica.

Obeah   African religion brought to the Caribbean.

Oil-down   Stew dish that has been cooked for a long period, also known as oileen or rundown, and made with a coconut milk base in Jamaica.

Pain d'epices   Thin biscuit.

Pan bati   Pancake made from cornmeal and flour.

Paratha   East Indian bread made on a griddle.

Pastie   Meat-stuffed pastry, also known as patty, pastellito, or pastecchi.

Pelau   One-pot meat and rice stew.

Pepperpot   Meat stew made with cassareep.

Pika   Hot pepper sauce used in the Dutch Caribbean that is made from onion and peppers pickled in vinegar.

Pikliz   Haitian hot pepper and vinegar marinade.

Pilon   Wooden mortar.

Pone   Baked pudding.

Pouile dudon   Chicken in coconut and sugar.

Pow   Small pork dumplings.

Pudding and souse   Sausage and pickled pig's feet. Souse is also a marinade for meat made from lime juice, pepper, and onions in the Bahamas.

Rastafarian   Member of the religious movement of Rastafarianism, which originated with Marcus Garvey.

Ratoon   Smaller harvest produced by the roots of sugarcane after the initial harvest.

Recaito   Another name for **sofrito**.

Riz djon djon   Rice dish made from Haitian black mushrooms.

Riz et pois colles   Haitian rice and bean dish.

Roasted meat kibby   Rice loaf stuffed with roasted meat, pine nuts, and onion.

Roti   East Indian bread.

Roucou   French term for **sofrito**.

Roux   Thickening base for stews made from browned flour.

Sada   East Indian bread made on a griddle.

Salamongundy   Cold salad made from various meats, fish, and condiments.

Sancocho   Puerto Rican beef stew.

Sankotch   Coconut milk stew.

Santeria   Pantheistic Yoruban religion brought to Caribbean.

Sauce chien   Hot pepper sauce.

Seasonin   Mixture of herbs and spices used in cooking, also known as sisonin.

Seining   Fishing with a large net.

Serenata   Salt fish marinated with sweet peppers.

Shark-and-bake   Shark steak served on two pieces of bread like a sandwich.

Sofrito   Seasoning mixture.

Sopa de gallo   Soup made from water and brown sugar.

Sopa di piska   Soup made from various kinds of fish.

Sopito   Fish and coconut soup made with salt meat.

Sousing   Manner of preparing pickled fish or meats.

Souskai   Manner of marinating unripe fruits and vegetables.

Stamp-and-go   Fish fritter.

Sullabub   Dessert made from white wine and brandy cream sauce topped with whipped cream and cherries.

Surullitos   Fried cornmeal slices.

Tawa   Type of griddle brought by Indian immigrants to the Caribbean.

Ti-malice   Haitian hot pepper sauce.

Tortilla española   Egg omelet made with potatoes and onions.

Tostones   Fried plantain chips.

Totoes   Gingerbread cookie.

Tourments d'amour   Coconut tart.

Voodoo   African religion practiced in the Caribbean.

Resource Guide

RECOMMENDED READING

Hillman, Richard, and Thomas J. D'Agostino, eds. *Understanding the Contemporary Caribbean*. Boulder, Colo.: Lynne Rienner, 2003.

Macpherson, John. *Caribbean Lands*. Trinidad and Jamaica: Longman Caribbean, 1963.

Mintz, Sidney, and Sally Price. *Caribbean Contours*. Baltimore, Md.: Johns Hopkins University Press, 1985.

Rogozinski, Jan. *A Brief History of the Caribbean from the Arawak and the Carib to the Present*. New York: Facts on File, 1992.

Sheller, Mimi. *Consuming the Caribbean*. New York: Routledge, 2003.

Wilson, Samuel, ed. *The Indigenous People of the Caribbean*. Gainesville: University of Florida Press, 1997.

COOKBOOKS

Barrow, Errol, and Kendal A. Lee. *Privilege Cooking in the Caribbean*. London: Macmillan, 1988.

Bladholm, Linda. *Latin and Caribbean Grocery Stores Demystified*. Los Angeles, Calif.: Renaissance Books, 2001.

Bourne, M. J., G. W. Lennox, and S. A. Seddon. *Fruits and Vegetable of the Caribbean*. London: Macmillan, 1988.

Brooks, Robert and Kara. *Paradise Found: The People, Restaurants and Recipes of St. Barthélemy*. Eastford, Conn.: Buckley Lane Press, 2003.

Brown, Charles Adolphus Thorburn. *Busha Browne's Indispensable Compendium of Traditional Jamaican Cookery*. Kingston, Jamaica: The Mills Press, 1993.

Cabanillas, Berta, and Carmen Ginorio. *Puerto Rican Dishes*. San Juan: Editorial de la Universidad de Puerto Rico, 1974.

Demers, John. *Caribbean Cooking*. New York: HPBooks, 1997.

———. *The Food of Jamaica*. Singapore: Periplus, 1999.

Dewitt, Dave, and Mary Jane Wilan. *Callaloo, Calypso and Carnival: The Cuisine of Trinidad and Tobago*. Freedom, Calif.: Crossing Press, 1993.

Donaldson, Enid. *The Real Taste of Jamaica*. Toronto: Warwick Publishing, 2000.

Elbert, Virginie F., and George Elbert. *Down-Island Caribbean Cookery*. New York: Simon and Schuster, 1991.

Grant, Rosamund. *Caribbean and African Cooking*. New York: Interlink Books, 1988.

———. *Cooking of the Caribbean*. London: Lorenz Books, 1999.

Hafner, Dorinda. *Dorinda's Taste of the Caribbean: African-Influenced Recipes from the Islands*. Berkeley, Calif.: Ten Speed Press, 1996.

Harris, Dunstan. *Island Barbecue*. San Francisco, Calif.: Chronicle Books, 1995.

———. *Island Cooking: Recipes from the Caribbean*. Freedom, Calif.: Crossing Press, 1988.

Harris, Jessica B. *Sky Juice and Flying Fish: Traditional Caribbean Cooking*. New York: Fireside, 1991.

Idone, Christopher. *Cooking Caribe*. New York: Panache Press, 1992.

Illsley, Linda. *Food and Festivals of the Caribbean*. Austin, Tex.: Raintree Steck-Vaughn, 1999.

Lady Darling. *Many Tastes of the Bahamas*. Nassau, Bahamas: Caribbean Productions, 2001.

Mackie, Christine. *Life and Food in the Caribbean*. New York: New Amsterdam, 1991.

———. *Trade Winds: Caribbean Cooking* (1987). Bristol: Longdunn, 1996.

Mackley, Lesley. *The Book of Caribbean Cooking*. New York: HPBooks, 2000.

McKenley, Yvonne. *A Taste of the Caribbean*. New York: Thomson Learning, 1995.

Morgan, Jinx, and Jefferson Morgan. *The Sugar Mill Caribbean Cookbook*. Boston: Harvard Common Press, 1996.

O'Higgins, María Josefa Lluriá de. *A Taste of Old Cuba*. New York: HarperCollins, 1994.

Ortiz, Elizabeth Lambert. *The Complete Book of Caribbean Cooking*. New York: Ballantine Books, 1973.

Ovide, Stéphanie. *French Caribbean Cuisine*. New York: Hippocrene Books, 2002.

Paraïso, Aviva. *Caribbean Food and Drink*. New York: Bookwright, 1989.

Parkinson, Rosemary. *Culinaria The Caribbean: A Culinary Discovery*. Köln: Könemann, 1999.

Perucca-Ramírez, and Julio J. Ramirez. *El Cocodrilo's Cookbook*. New York: Macmillan, 1996.

Pitkin, Julia M. *Great Chefs of the Caribbean*. Nashville, Tenn.: Cumberland House, 2000.

Raichlen, Steven. *The Caribbean Pantry Cookbook*. New York: Artisan, 1995.

Randelman, Mary Urrutia, and Joan Schwartz. *Memories of a Cuban Kitchen: More Than 200 Classic Recipes*. New York: Wiley, 1992.

Robinson, Jan. *Bahama Mama's Cooking*. St. Thomas: Ship to Shore, 1996.

Slater, Mary. *Cooking the Caribbean Way* (1965). New York: Hippocrene Books, 1998.

Springer, Rita G. *Caribbean Cookbook*. London: Pan Books, 1975.

Sullivan, Caroline. *Classic Jamaican Cooking: Traditional Recipes and Herbal Remedies*. London: Serif, 2003.

Willinsky, Helen. *Jerk: Barbecue from Jamaica*. Freedom, Calif.: Crossing Press, 1990.

Wolfe, Linda. *The Cooking of the Caribbean Islands* (Foods of the World). New York: Time Life Books, 1970.

Yurnet-Thomas, Mirta, and the Thomas family. *A Taste of Haiti*. New York: Hippocrene Books, 2002.

FILM

Great Chefs of the Caribbean (1999). A set of cooking demonstration videos produced by the Discovery Channel; published separately as a cookbook.

The Greening of Cuba (1996). A short film produced by the U.S. Institute for Food and Development Policy about the history of organic agriculture in Cuba during the 1990s.

Life and Debt (2002). A documentary film about Jamaican culture produced by Stephanie Black, that includes substantial footage of various aspects of Jamaican agriculture.

Marketing What We Grow (1963). A documentary about farming in Jamaica that depicts policies enacted in the 1960s to lessen the negative effects of export-led development on Jamaican agriculture.

Sugar Cane Alley (1984). A film that depicts the life of workers on a sugar cane plantation and their hopes of giving their children a better future through education; directed by Euzhan Palcy and starring Darling Legitimus, Garry Cadenat, Douta Seck, and Joby Bernabe.

ORGANIZATIONS

Caribbean Agricultural Research and Development Institute. University of West Indies Campus, St. Augustine, Trinidad, West Indies.

The Caribbean Culinary Federation. 1000 Ponce de León Ave., 5th Floor San
    Juan, Puerto Rico, 00907.
Caribbean Food Crops Society (CFCS). c/o Dr Kofi Boateng, University of the
    Virgin Islands, RR02, Box 10000, Kingshill, St. Croix, U.S. Virgin Islands
    00850.
Caribbean Food & Nutrition Institute. Jamaica Centre, POB 140, Mona 7,
    Kingston, Jamaica.

WEB SITES

http://www.caribbeanchoice.com/main.asp. This is mostly a travel-based site but
    also offers great discussion boards on various aspects of Caribbean food
    and cooking.
http://www.caribbeanfoodemporium.co.uk/sitemap.htm. This site contains ex-
    haustive and extensive information on Caribbean food both in Caribbean
    territories and internationally.
http://www.caribbeansupplies.com/shop/products.html. This site sells many Ca-
    ribbean items from handicrafts to food supplies and ingredients.
http://www.globalgourmet.com/. This site contains comprehensive information
    about Jamaican and Caribbean food culture with recipes, a glossary of
    terms (called a menu guide), and historical and cultural information re-
    lated to Caribbean cuisine.
http://www.gracefoods.com. A site run by a Jamaican food distribution company,
    Grace, Kennedy Co., with recipes and product information.
http://www.islandflave.com. A South Florida site that includes recipes and infor-
    mation about popular culture of the Caribbean.
http://www.recipes4us.co.uk. A British site dedicated to international cuisines.
    Their West Indies category contains recipes and a brief culinary history.
http://www.unichef.com/caribgloss.htm. This link provides a great glossary of Ca-
    ribbean foods, along with preparation information.
http://www.wifglobal.com/Caribbeanfoods.htm. A site that offers a variety of Ca-
    ribbean cooking products for sale.

Bibliography

Alleyne, George. *Whither Caribbean Health: A Study*. Black Rock, St. Michael, Barbados: West Indian Commission Secretariat, 1992.

Accaria-Zavala, Diane. "Breaking the Spell of Our Hallucinated Lucidity: Surveying the Caribbean Self within Hollywood Cinema." In *The Cultures of the Hispanic Caribbean*, ed. Conrad James and John Perivolaris. Warwick, England: Warwick University Press, 2001. pp. 226–40.

Ahmed, Belal, and Sultana Afroz. *The Political Economy of Food and Agriculture in the Caribbean*. Kingston, Jamaica: Ian Randle, 1996.

Allsopp, Jeannette. *The Caribbean Multilingual Dictionary of Flora, Fauna and Foods*. Kingston, Jamaica: Arawak Publications, 2003.

Benjamin, Medea, Joseph Collins, and Michael Scott. *No Free Lunch: Food and Revolution in Cuba Today*. San Francisco: Food First Books, 1984.

Brereton, Bridget and Kevin A. Yelvington, eds. *The Colonial Caribbean in Transition: Essays on Postemancipation and Social History*. Gainesville, University Press of Florida, 1999.

Buck, Wilbur F. *Agriculture and Trade of the Caribbean Region*. Washington, D.C.: U.S. Department of Agriculture Economic Research Service, 1971.

Clarke, Austin. *Pig Tails in Breadfruit: The Rituals of Slave Food*. Toronto: Random House, 1999.

Dewitt, Dave, and Mary Jane Wilan. *Callaloo, Calypso and Carnival: The Cuisine of Trinidad and Tobago*. Freedom, Calif.: Crossing Press, 1993.

Dunn, Richard S. *Sugar and Slaves: The Rise of the Planter Class in the English West Indies, 1624–1713*. Chapel Hill: University of North Carolina Press, 1972.

Eyre, L. Alan. "How Long Can Jamaica Feed Itself?" *Cajanus* 3, no. 2 (April 1970), pp. 77–85.

Gardner, Marjorie. "Street Foods in Papine, St. Andrew, Jamaica: Their Role in the Foodservice Industry." Southwest/Texas Regional Popular Culture Association/American Culture Association. San Antonio, Texas. April 8, 2004.

Gilmore, John. *Faces of the Caribbean*. London: Latin America Bureau, 2000.

Hagley, Knox E. "Nutrition and Health in the Developing World: The Caribbean Experience" *Proceedings of the Nutrition Society* 52, vol. 1 (February 1993), pp. 183–87.

———. "An Overview of the Problem." *Cajanus* 23, no. 1 (1990): pp. 8–13.

Health Conditions in the Caribbean. Washington, D.C.: Pan American Health Organization, 1997.

Higman, B. W. "Cookbooks and Caribbean Cultural Identity: An English-Language Hors D'Oeuvre." *New West Indian Guide/Nieuwe West-Indische Gids* 72, nos. 1 and 2 (1998).

Hillman, Richard, and Thomas J. D'Agostino, eds. *Understanding the Contemporary Caribbean*. Boulder, Colo.: Lynne Rienner, 2003.

Inter-American Institute for Cooperation on Agriculture. *Regional Overview of Food Security in Latin America and the Caribbean with a Focus on Agricultural Research, Technology Transfer and Application*. San José, Costa Rica. (1991).

Katzin, Margaret Fisher. "The Business of Higglering in Jamaica." In *Peoples and Cultures of the Caribbean*, ed. Michael Horowitz. New York: Natural History Press, 1971.

Kiple, Kenneth F. *The Caribbean Slave: A Biological History*. Cambridge: Cambridge University Press, 1984.

Landman-Bouges, J. "Rastafarian Food Habits." *Cajanus* 9, no. 4 (1977), pp. 228–34.

Mackie, Christine. *Life and Food in the Caribbean*. New York: New Amsterdam, 1991.

———. *Trade Winds: Caribbean Cooking* (1987). Bristol: Longdunn, 1996.

Macpherson, John. *Caribbean Lands*. Trinidad and Jamaica: Longman Caribbean, 1963.

May, Jacques M., and Donna L. McLellan. *The Ecology of Malnutrition in the Caribbean*. (Studies in Medical Geography, vol. 12). New York: Hafner Press, 1973.

Mintz, Sidney W. *Sweetness and Power: The Place of Sugar in Modern History*. New York: Penguin, 1985.

———. *Tasting Food, Tasting Freedom: Excursion into Eating, Culture, and the Past*. Boston, Beacon Press, 1996.

———. *Worker in the Cane: A Puerto Rican Life History*. New York: W. W. Norton & Company, 1974.

Mintz, Sidney, and Sally Price. *Caribbean Contours*. Baltimore, Md.: Johns Hopkins University Press, 1985.

Newsome, Lee A. and Elizabeth S. Wing. *On Land and Sea: Native American Uses of Biological Resources in the West Indies.* Tuscaloosa, Al.: University of Alabama Press, 2004.

Nutritional Anemias in Latin America and the Caribbean. Washington, D.C.: Pan American Health Organization, 1968.

Olazagasti, Ignacio. "The Material Culture of the Taino Indians." In *Indigenous Peoples of the Caribbean,* ed. Samuel M. Wilson. Gainesville: University Press of Florida, 1997.

Pascoe, Natalie T. *Caribbean Spice: A Traveller's Guide to Cultural Festivals and Events.* Silver Springs, Md.: DePas Publishing, 1998.

Price, Richard. "Caribbean Fishing and Fisherman: A Historical Sketch." *American Anthropologist* 68, (1966), pp. 1363–83.

Rogozinski, Jan. *A Brief History of the Caribbean from the Arawak and the Carib to the Present.* New York: Facts on File, 1992.

Sandiford, Keith A. *The Cultural Politics of Sugar: Caribbean Slavery and Narratives of Colonialism.* Cambridge: Cambridge University Press, 2000.

Senior, Olive. *Working Miracles: Women of the English-speaking Caribbean.* Kingston, Jamaica: Heinemann, 1991.

Sheller, Mimi. *Consuming the Caribbean.* London: Routledge, 2003.

Sinha, D. P. "Changing Patterns of Food, Nutrition and Health in the Caribbean." *Nutrition Research* 6, vol. 15, (June 1995), pp. 899–938.

Strachan, Ian Gregory. *Paradise and Plantation: Tourism and Culture in the Anglophone Caribbean.* Charlottesville: University of Virginia Press, 2002.

Tanasescu, Mihaela et al. "Biobehavioral Factors Are Associated with Obesity in Puerto Rican Children." Journal of Nutrition, 130 (2000), pp. 1734–42.

Tinker, Irene. *Street Foods: Urban Food and Employment in Developing Countries.* New York: Oxford University Press, 1997.

Wilson, Samuel, ed. *The Indigenous People of the Caribbean.* Gainesville: University of Florida Press, 1997.

Wolfe, Linda. *The Cooking of the Caribbean Islands.* (Foods of the World.) New York: Time Life Books, 1970.

Index

About the Author

LYNN MARIE HOUSTON is a food historian who has written frequently on food in the Caribbean.

**Recent Titles in
Food Culture around the World**